How To Be Whole Again

Defeat Fear of Abandonment, Anxiety, and Self-Doubt. Be an Emotionally Mature Adult Despite Coming From a Dysfunctional Family

By Zoe McKey

Copyright © 2020 by Zoe McKey. All rights reserved.

No part of this publication may be reproduced, stored in a retrieval system, or transmitted in any form or by any means, electronic, mechanical, photocopying, recording, scanning or otherwise, except as permitted under Section 107 or 108 of the 1976 United States Copyright Act, without the prior written permission of the author.

Limit of Liability/ Disclaimer of Warranty: The author makes no representations or warranties with respect to the accuracy or completeness of the contents of this work and specifically disclaims all warranties, including without limitation warranties of fitness for a particular purpose. No warranty may be created or extended by sales or promotional materials. The advice and recipes contained herein may not be suitable for everyone. This work is sold with the understanding that the author is not engaged in rendering medical, legal or other professional advice or services. If professional assistance is required, the services of a competent professional person should be sought. The author shall not be liable for damages arising herefrom. The fact that an individual, organization of website is referred to in this work as a citation and/or potential source of further information does not mean that the author endorses the information the individual, organization to website may provide or recommendations they/it may make. Further, readers should be aware that Internet websites listed in this work might have changed or disappeared between when this work was written and when it is read.

For general information on the products and services or to obtain technical support, please contact the author.

CREATED BY

ZOE MCKEY

SELF-DISCOVERY
~Starter Kit~

Thank you for choosing my book! I would like to show my appreciation for the trust you gave me by giving a **FREE GIFT** to you!

To download your gift, visit:

www.zoemckey.com

The kit shares *10 key practices to help you to:*

- *discover your true self,*
- *find your life areas that need improvement,*
- *find self-forgiveness,*
- *become better at socializing,*
- *lead a life of gratitude and purpose.*

The kit contains extra actionable worksheets with practice exercises for deeper learning.

Table of Contents

Introduction 11

Chapter 1: My Story 23

Chapter 2: Uncovering Emotional Immaturity 55

Chapter 3: Defense Mechanisms 83

Chapter 4: On Boundaries 107

Chapter 5: Narcissism 143

Chapter 6: Gaslighting 159

Chapter 7: Abandonment Issues 173

Chapter 8: The Mind-Changing Magic of Meditation 189

Chapter 9: On Shaming, Blaming, and Criticizing 217

Chapter 10: Anxiously Yours…................... 231

A Final Thought… 245

Before You Go… 251

References 265

Endnotes 269

Introduction

I was sitting at the window of my maternal grandparents' house watching my father's gray car disappearing in the distance. I was four or five. My parents just opened a new store in a city 80 miles away from the village where I was staying and growing up. My parents were new in the professional lighting industry, so they needed all their time and attention on getting the business started. It was going to provide a future for the family and for me, their only child. Of course, I didn't understand all the adult implications of being busy opening a business at such a young age. All I wanted was to have my mom and dad around.

Maybe it sounds odd to say this—as the book is about healing and maturing from traumas suffered in childhood—but I was mostly a happy child. My parents loved me. They wanted me. My maternal grandparents also loved me. They took good care of me as I was growing up. My grandmother was a retired elementary school teacher, bored out of her mind from staying at home. Having more free time than ever before, she mostly invested it in incessant cleaning and my education. Thanks to her I could read, write, count, and I knew all European countries, their capitals, and the rivers crossing each capital by the age of four. My grandparents eagerly showed me off to relatives, friends, and pretty much everyone who set foot in our home. I felt like a little circus monkey but I loved the attention. Especially that of my parents. I couldn't wait for them to come home—to the village—every weekend so I could prove to them how much they were missing out on by not being with me. I thought if I only knew a little bit more, if I sang just a little bit better, or if I cried just a little bit louder, they'd stay. But they never did.

As I mentioned before, my story is not a terribly traumatic one, but emotional abandonment, neglect, and experiences of lacking are not necessarily the result of violence, sexual assault, addiction, or death.

My story has much more covert negative elements in it, which I dare say, is more common than the stories that utterly shock you. But we don't know about stories like mine because people don't speak about them. I think personal stories work like advertisements: if there is nothing sensationally good or bad about them, they won't get publicity. No one pays attention to them. Even I get sold on the belief that my story is not worth mentioning because there are much worse out there. I was almost ashamed to complain as I dreaded people's reactions; they would dismiss it as nothing, they would judge me or my loved ones, or they simply wouldn't care. Why bother, then?

As a child, a teenager, and even a young adult, I was silent about my story. I barely opened up about a fraction of it to my friends. Well-wishing positive psychology gurus teach us not to connect with people using our bucket of stuff. So I didn't. I didn't want to seem ungrateful, complaining, or worse... broken.

Can you relate? (I will ask this question frequently in this book.) Do you think you mostly stayed silent about the negative experiences that shaped your life? Or the positive ones, for that matter? What are your motivations for not sharing? If you share, are you aware what your intention is behind that choice? Do you seek understanding from others? Do you wish to be excused for some of your shortcomings by playing the victim card? Do you share out of desperation? Do you share to ease your mind? Would you like to find answers? Do you share because you feel in a safe space? We choose to talk—or not talk—about ourselves due to various motivations. I think it is very important to know what those motivations are before we truly start working on our childhood baggage. Please take a moment to think about what yours are.

I held my "non-sharing policy" firmly until the age of 27. Let me stop here for a second. I know that age and credibility are strongly tied together. But age in the case of that big aha moment in life is a relative number. I feel extremely grateful for being so young when I had my breakthrough realization about "who I was" and "why I was that way." According to research, most people get to this point somewhere in their mid to late thirties—even in their forties, otherwise known as the midlife crisis. Some people gain awareness about these questions as soon as their late teens (those lucky younglings). And some never get such an aha moment and live their six, seven, or nine decades on this Earth without knowing the answer to the questions "Who am I?" and "Why am I this way?" So, age is just a number, my dear. If you are younger or older than I am, it doesn't matter. The earlier you start the better, but—and a big but is coming—just because you discover some truths about your upbringing, and its consequences to your life thus far at any age, it doesn't mean your job's done there. No.

The cycle of awareness, confusion, anger, acceptance, and forgiveness has to be done and redone over and over again. The truths you get blessed enough to understand in your teens will be different than what you understand in your twenties, thirties, forties, and so on. The lightness or heaviness of our childhood baggage is like Prometheus' liver. It doesn't matter how many times we eat it, curse it, therapy it out of our system, it grows back every once in a while. It will be smaller, and less painful, of course, but it is a baggage that we ultimately carry to the grave. But it makes a huge difference how we carry this bag; will we casually throw it over our shoulder while we walk the flat road, or will we struggle to pull it up Everest? That's the difference we can make about our past. And it's all the difference in the world.

We all have been dealt bags to carry. Some were blessed to get a neat little clutch, some of us got luggage so big that no sensible airline would carry it without extra charge—and one wheel is also missing. Whatever bag you got is not your fault. That's just life, and life isn't fair (a fairy just died now that I wrote that), so don't wait for life to compensate you for your losses; it is not a zero-sum game. In my teens and even my early twenties I believed life owed me something for all the hardships I had to go through and thus—unfortunately—I took the help of many people for granted. I lived without showing the proper gratitude to those who held my hand along my bumpy road. Today I know I made a mistake, and it took me some time to forgive myself for it. But hey, having these kinds of realizations and doing better after them is called growth.

But back to the bag we were dealt with... It is up to us to empty it and make it as user-friendly as possible—regardless if we have the rat purse or the elephant coffin. We can all do better than to just give up and settle. It's our responsibility to make the best out of what we got.

Clutches are annoying; you need to hold them in one hand. Your job is to saw a handle on the clutch to be able to carry it without constantly sacrificing a hand. If you had the wheel-less trolley, you'd need to empty it, and then put some awesome 24K gold wheels on it so they'd slide like magic. As you can see, everyone has to do something with their bags. What I know for sure is that life doesn't dispense padded, aerodynamic, lightweight Rimowa backpacks for anyone. Everyone has to craft their own version of that.

If we stick with the bag analogy, I think I was given a tote. Not a fancy one, not an O bag or a Longchamp. I got a medium-sized tote with those incredibly uncomfortable straps which would leave red and blue bruises on your shoulder for days if you did some big-time grocery shopping. That kind of tote. Oh, and my tote had a big hole on the bottom. I will tell you the (w)hole story soon.

I was heavily debating for months whether or not I should tell you my story. As I mentioned above, before I had my big aha moment of "who I was" and "why I was that way," I didn't talk about my real story to anyone because I

19

didn't want to be a complainer, ungrateful, or seem broken. After my aha moment, I talked to my friends about my life. But for a while I was still uncertain on writing this book because… I thought that I had nothing to offer, that I might piss off people who faced much bigger traumas than I did. But I was so wrong. First, I was wrong to stay silent for 27 years to the people closest to me. And I would have been so wrong if I didn't write this book and share with you my story and how I overcame the odds I was given.

My story matters. Your story matters. Every story does. We all carry scars, and our scars hurt us, sabotage us, and can throw us to the deepest pits of despair. And the worst thing we can do, heed my words, the worst thing we can do is to stay silent, to minimize our personal traumas, to compare them to those who had it worse, and then decide not to do anything about ours. Even though someone got their leg chopped off, you will also bleed to death with your thumb off. You need to heal your thumb. And that person has to heal their leg. The two things are not mutually exclusive. There is no trauma competition here—just people who wish to be their best, mature, adult selves despite and because of their early experiences.

There is an element here—an emotion, more precisely—that keeps most of us, the (oh, I hate this word, but it's legitimate to use it here) victims of smaller or greater traumas, silent. And that's shame. Shame that we are broken, that we aren't and can't be enough, that we're fundamentally flawed, marked, infected…

The antidote to shame is sharing—according to experts, and also in my experience. "Where there is honesty and vulnerability, shame can't survive," says Brene Brown, the international best-selling author and shame and vulnerability researcher. Sharing is healing. But heed

Brown's caveat, "If we share our shame story with the wrong person, they can easily become one more piece of flying debris in an already dangerous storm." So sharing with the right people is essential to creating a safe space.

I will take a leap of faith to share my story with you. Based on the lessons I learned through therapy, journaling, reading more than 70 books on the topic, and talking about life experiences with people in more than 35 countries I wish to offer you comfort, validation, life-changing advice, a bittersweet and fun read, emotional support, presence, and the experience that you are not alone.

I'm not a professional therapist or psychologist, so please take the advice I share for what it is: the experience of a regular girl who deeply wishes to help you because she knows that what you're going through is hard and that you have the potential to heal.

Chapter 1: My Story

Let's go back to where I started in the previous chapter. Once upon a time…

"I was sitting in the window of my maternal grandparents' house watching my father's grey car disappearing in the distance. I was four or five. My parents just opened a new store in a city 80 miles away from the village where I was staying and growing up. My parents were new in the professional lighting industry so they needed all their time and attention on getting the business started. It was going to provide a future for the family and to me, their only child. Of course, I didn't understand all the adult implications of being busy opening a business at such a young age. All I wanted was to have my mom and dad around…"

And all I could feel when I saw their car pull out of my grandparents' driveway was a deep sense of unimportance. "My parents don't care about me because they go back to the business every Sunday evening and they don't leave until Friday evening. It doesn't matter how nice of a drawing I make, how good of a puppet show I perform with my dolls, how awesome dance choreography I prepare with my little friends, how many letters I can write and read at the age of four, they still leave me every Friday. I must not be good enough to make them stay."

I am not good enough to make them stay. That is why they leave. Because I am inadequate, therefore unlovable, therefore unimportant.

People will always leave me unless I become good enough.

There you go. The first belief I adopted about myself at an age I can't remember much about. I was not good or important enough. I remember the fear of abandonment, the shame of failing to make my parents stay, the excessive people-pleasing activities I went through to wow my parents into staying each weekend, and the bitterness on my grandma's face when I threw a tantrum each Sunday telling her how much I missed my parents. "Don't you love me too?" she would ask sadly. Of course I did, but she was there—so I took that for granted. Yet I felt extremely guilty for making her sad. So after the age of five I stopped crying when my parents left. The adults thought, *finally, she is a big girl now.* Little did they know that I was now juggling with two heavy emotions, of not being enough and being a bad person if I expressed my sorrow. My habit of explosion only transformed into implosion.

You know, for a long time I didn't understand how these seemingly small events influenced my entire life. Only recently could I see the correlation between why I struggle sharing my problems—especially negative ones—with others, why I am a people pleaser to the core, why I get stuck repeatedly in emotionally (and even physically) abusive long-term relationships one after the other, and my parents leaving me each week peppered with my grandmother's emotional blackmailing.

These early abandonment scars led me to beg one of my ex-boyfriends not to slice his own neck ten years later, and cry and beg another ex-boyfriend to love me while he pulled away in disgust twenty years later. I dated both of these men for almost four years each. The aforementioned events were not the mark of our breakup. In other words, I had a high tolerance for all sort of emotional, psychological abuse just to keep them with me. To not lose them. As my therapist told me, I developed an incredibly high tolerance for emotional abuse out of a fear of abandonment.

Retrospectively, making this connection is not rocket science and it all makes sense now. But back then when I was dating them, it didn't. And it was terrifying to live in these relationships. I felt insecure, anxious, constantly walking on eggshells, and I waited for the proverbial gray car to pull out the driveway at any moment. Today I understand why I chose these guys. They were generally cold, hard-working men, to whom I never came first, and who never made me feel safe, wanted, and good enough. They were highly critical of me on one hand and overconfident on the other hand. And all I did day and night was try to prove to them my worth. So they wouldn't leave me. I felt like trying to fill a tote that had a hole in its bottom. I felt the same way with my parents every weekend.

I don't mean to give the wrong impression. My ex-partners were not bad people. Yet together we created a terrible dynamic. Just as I attracted them based on my own childhood wounds, they also attracted me based on their own. We had a lot to learn from each other, and hopefully we can all grow from our shared experience. Those eight years I spent with them were hard lessons but net-positive learning curves. Without those experiences today I wouldn't know what my shortcomings are, what I absolutely refuse to accept in a relationship, and I also have a more clear idea about what I want.

My Mom

It was a warm September night and I was rolling around in my bed in Timisoara, Romania. I was eight and had been living with my parents for the second year. From the age of five my parents started experimenting with keeping me with them for a longer time. But after a few weeks of being mostly with nannies and babysitters, my mother decided that I was better off with my grandparents. So they moved me back to the village. Then a few months passed, my mom started being restless again about not having me around, and as they had a less busy season at the shop, they moved me back to Timisoara. Then a few weeks passed, and again, they took me back to my grandparents. This dynamic went on to the point where I had to start school. As my parents wanted to provide me with the best education, they decided to move me full time to the "big" city. When I was a first grader, my grandparents also moved up to town to live with us so that I could get used to the big change more smoothly.

I loved that year of my life—I think that was the best year of my childhood, having everyone dear to me under the same roof. But to my parents and grandparents it was more like a nightmare, being cramped in a three-bedroom apartment in a block of flats. The idea was for my grandparents to soon move into a new house in the suburbs of Timisoara my parents were building up from scratch. However, God dealt different cards to us. Our business started going poorly so my parents were forced to sell the suburban house and my grandparents immediately moved back to their village.

And there I was lying in my bed on a warm September night, about to start second grade at school, thinking about how much I missed my grandparents, when something unexpected happened. To this day cold chills run down my spine as I vaguely remember the memory. It was a frightening, sharp, long scream in the silent evening. It was my mom's voice. Fear froze my limbs as I was debating what could have happened. Did a burglar just kill my mom? Was it my dad? What should I do? But before I could think about it for too long, my door flew open and banged against the wall with a loud slam. My mom was standing in the door, but somehow it wasn't her. Her usually organized, hairdresser-blown hair was tangled, her eyes bulging, and her dress hung oddly on her slim figure. "The world's end is coming, we need to leave," she said in an eerie voice, and before I knew it, she yanked me out of the bed and aggressively pulled me out to the street.

My dad just arrived home in those moments and tried to take control of the situation by trying to yank me back from my mother and calming her down. It must have been a comical sight for our neighbors, my parents pulling me back and forth, both yelling. When I could escape I ran back to my room and locked the door. Little did I know that this was the first night of my new reality.

A few months later, my mom was diagnosed with schizophrenia. In the beginning (and here I'm talking about a few years) she rejected to take her medication as she thought there was nothing wrong with her. When she finally started taking her medication, she developed type 2 diabetes which slowly brought her down physically. Schizophrenia took care of her brilliant mind.

My mom was considered "gifted" all her life. She was one of those super-smart people, geniuses (not uncommon among people with schizophrenia, as I later learned). She excelled in her studies and she was the mastermind behind our business, which was actually very successful until she started losing her mind to this insidious illness. My mom was respected by many. She was a pretty, stylish, modern woman. I witnessed her transform into someone unrecognizable in a time frame that seemed like a blink of an eye. She was in a very dark place for a decade. There were some small windows of time when she was herself, but most of the time she was mumbling incoherently or running savagely screaming on the streets. Her symptoms only deteriorated further when our business went bankrupt a few years later.

I spent eight years of my life living with my parents and out of these eight years my mom was ill seven. Naturally this situation forged a stronger bond between my dad and me. He became my best friend. (Which is not a good sign in parenting, but as a child I didn't know that.) My dad has a kind and generous heart. He is playful, fun to be around, and has a carefree personality. He is also emotionally immature and somewhat self-absorbed. He takes great pride in "not growing up" and having the spirit of a young person. I tend to think about him as Peter Pan, you know, forty years later. I was very close with my dad until I started maturing emotionally. I think we had a natural connection in my teenage years because we were at the same emotional developmental stage. When I became a "boring adult" we mutually lost interest in each other. But in those seven years when my mom was sick, my dad was by my side, and I'm very grateful for that.

Just as schizophrenia trapped my mom's mind, Ponzi schemes trapped my dad's. The "get rich fast, or die trying" pyramid schemes[1] were the new fad in post-communist Eastern Europe at that time. There was very little internet access back in the early 2000s, and frankly, these pyramid schemes sounded exactly like the treasure at the end of the rainbow. And so my dad started his never-ending treasure hunt.

We had more properties at that point and ended up selling one after the other to make ends meet and to have some cash to invest into the next pyramid scheme. Needless to say, my family ran out of money incredibly quickly. My mom

---

[1] If you are unfamiliar with the term, briefly, "a pyramid scheme is a business model that recruits members via a promise of payments or services for enrolling others into the scheme, rather than supplying investments or sale of products. As recruiting multiplies, recruiting becomes quickly impossible, and most members are unable to profit; as such, pyramid schemes are unsustainable and often illegal." Smith, Rodney K. (1984). Multilevel Marketing. Baker Publishing Group. p. 45. ISBN 0-8010-8243-9.

became very desperate as my dad wasted all our fortune and accumulated some debt. She still was the responsible adult in the family. Still she was the one who made sure our bills were paid, and the tax reports filed.

I wish I could share more about this period of my life but I hardly have any memories. As we discussed with my therapist, this might be my brain's defense mechanism against the repeated trauma of seeing my mother go rogue so often; some kind of amnesia due to trauma.

How did I feel about having my mother while not having her? The best I could describe the feeling is with Cheryl Strayed's words—a bit edited.

> "I didn't get to grow up and pull away from her and bitch about her with my friends and confront her

about the things I'd wished she'd done differently and then get older and understand that she had done the best she could and realize that what she had done was pretty damn good and take her fully back into my arms again. Her ~~death~~ *illness* had obliterated that. It had obliterated me. It had cut me short at the ~~very height~~ *beginning* of my youthful arrogance. It had forced me to instantly grow up and forgive her every motherly fault at the same time that it kept me forever a child, my life both ended and begun in that premature place where we'd left off. She was my mother, but I was motherless. I was trapped by her, but utterly alone. She would always be the empty bowl that no one could fill. I'd have to fill it myself again and again and again."

My parents (mostly my father) had to make a difficult decision, as the home above my head didn't provide enough food and emotional safety—they sent me to a boarding school in Hungary at the age of fifteen. They wanted the best for me; a private school in Hungary sounded like our best option at that moment. Hungary was considered a more evolved, ahead-of-its-time post-communist country than Romania. In the eyes of my parents they made a great decision by giving me the chance of a better education, and thus a better life. In my eyes, I was just ditched again and unwanted.

I stopped feeling sorry for myself a long time ago. I wasn't the real victim having a mom with schizophrenia. My mom was. Is. And yet she isn't. She is so strong! She is the adult at home to this day. She takes care of my dad rather than vice versa (even though my dad is officially her caregiver). She made peace with her illness and invested her conscious time in reading and in art. She draws amazingly. She was an architect before becoming a businesswoman, so she explored her drawing skills inspired by her madness and she did some amazing artwork. She even had an exhibition about a year ago.

It might be wishful thinking or just me growing up, but I think my mom is doing better the past years. She hardly ever mumbles, she hasn't screamed or run outside for years. She is struggling more with the negative symptoms of her illness nowadays, which is a lack of motivation to do anything. But she always cheers up when I'm around. And that warms my heart. As distant as we were for almost twenty years, we are getting just as close now. I thought I had nothing in common with my mom when I was younger. And it was true. I had to gain some maturity to understand the beauty in her sorrow, the wisdom in her gentle advice, how great of a human being she is, and how lucky I am that she is my mom.

For years I wished I had a different mom. Someone who makes sandwiches for her child for school instead of showing up screaming in her pajamas, who could give me advice on sex, and boys, and how to use a tampon—instead of someone who looks so sad. Someone who tells me to be patient, loving, and trust God.

But today I can see how right she was and how good of an example she has been to me by staying strong and not giving up in a state where most people would just put a bullet through their crazy brain. After both of us went through our own dark journey and came out at the better end of it, we can talk for hours while making sandwiches. We talk about sex, and boys, and how to use a tampon, and also about how to be a kind, patient, and loving person in the world.

My mom taught me the best lesson about patience. It's not about patience, it's about what you do while you're being patient.

My Dad

My first year in Hungary was a living hell and my worst year ever. I couldn't expect financial aid from my parents. I was the poor, smart girl with a scholarship among a bunch of wealthy but less education-invested kids. I was the outlier.

That year both of my grandparents died three months apart. They were the people who practically raised me. I had more memories with them than I had with my parents. And I was far away when they passed. I remember I never replied to my grandmother's last letter because I was too busy trying to fit in and impress the people at my school who were not interested in accepting me. I felt guilty about not responding to that letter for more than a decade.

I couldn't really process their death that year. Or the next. Or the next. I can only quote Cheryl Strayed again:

> "Grief is tremendous, but love is bigger. You are grieving because you loved truly. The beauty in that is greater than the bitterness of death. Allowing this into your

42

consciousness will not keep you from suffering, but it will help you survive the next day."

When I truly internalized the message of this quote and I started feeling incredibly lucky for having my grandparents in my life so closely for so long, the grip of grief slowly subsided. So did my guilt. I wrote a letter to my grandmother apologizing to her for slacking in reaching out, telling her about my life, and thanking her for all that she had done for me—and my guilt subsided. I imagined her forgiving me for not writing her the letter in time and calling me "my dearest star" as she used to. I'm not a believer, but if heaven exists and our soul is eternal, I'm sure she is very happy, loves me a lot, and doesn't want me to feel guilty.

I know many of you suffer from enormous guilt because of words you didn't say, hugs you didn't share, and apologies you never uttered… The helplessness around our deceased loved ones can be perpetually crippling until we decide to forgive ourselves, ask for forgiveness in whatever form we can, and find consolation in the thought that our loved one wouldn't want us to suffer.

Not long after the shock of losing my grandparents, I received another. My mom and her brother decided to sell the house where I grew up in, the house of my grandparents. I felt so attached to that little village house, I thought that the walls kept my grandparents' spirits alive. Once, before the sale was finalized, I went back one last time to collect some personal items from the house. Weirdly, I felt nothing being there. There was no soul left in the familiar spaces. It was just a property now. Without my grandparents in it, there was nothing left there.

My mom and uncle decided to put the money they got for the house into a bank account which would give me about $130 every month, giving me a comfortable living aid. This amount doesn't sound like a lot of money, but given that I had a roof above my head (a dormitory), all I really needed was food and some clothes. In 2007 you could get around in Hungary with what I received. And it was supposed to be a secure income up until the year I finished my university degree. Why did I say it was supposed to? Because it never provided me security for longer than about four months.

My dad was bamboozled by another business opportunity and he decided to empty my account (being the legal beneficiary of my bank account until I turned 18) and invest all that money into this new pyramid scheme with the—I don't doubt—genuine hope to make that money back threefold and get rich quickly—and make everyone happy. Unfortunately, yet predictably, he lost all this money, ironically, on my birthday, sentencing me to almost ten years of true neediness and impoverishment. He never asked permission to take that money from anyone. He was defensive and emotionally manipulative when I asked him where did the money go, and when will he give it back? Month by month he promised that the next month he would send me money and return what he took away.

It was always the next month.

The more often he failed at keeping his promise, my insistence about the money raised. I couldn't legally work, yet I had bills to pay—like my cellphone, my public transportation ticket, and food.

My dad, being an impatient guy who hated nagging, often yelled back saying he couldn't believe all I wanted from him was money. "When I die, you shall see that there are more important things in this life than money." This was his go-to line—he knew I'd shut up if he said that.

I was ashamed of myself for being so money hungry. I felt sorry for my dad. I thought that it must have been hard for him having my mom ill, constantly losing money and lacking in life in general. I wanted to keep him safe, to not cause him more headache, so I never spoke to anyone about what he did. As far as my mom and my extended family were concerned, I had the money coming each month.

My uncle (the one who had forgone his parental inheritance for me) sometimes helped me with some money, my paternal grandparent did as well, but they were all convinced that I was an intemperate spendthrift, as they *knew* I had enough money for food.

I honestly don't even remember how I made ends meet those years. But thanks to the generous and selfless help of so many people, I made it. Sometimes I had to steal, sometimes give up all my pride and beg, sometimes I had to cry, or lie, or both. I made it. And until the age of 27 it never even occurred to me that so much mess can leave a mark on my psyche.

Stay on the Sunny Side…

"Hell no!" I yelled back at my mom about a year ago, deep in the period where I prematurely prided myself as being "aware." I was sobbingly complaining to my mom about my failing relationship with my latest ex. Let's call him LE for Latest Ex. He and I were a couple for almost four years by then. LE was kind and generous at his core but also hyper-critical and cold. We were singing the real-life song of ice and fire almost from the very beginning. I was emotional, warm, and passionate. He was logical, cold, and dispassionate. But we were crazy about each other in the beginning and committed way too early without questioning and exploring how compatible we actually were. Our differences—my still untreated childhood wounds, his total obliviousness about his wounds and his critical, unforgiving, and empathy-lacking nature—culminated in a dynamic where we brought the very worst out of each other. He actively rejected me as a woman, withholding his affections and love, but sticking around because... I'm not sure to this day why, but probably because some part of him couldn't let the idea of us go. We lived in this emotionless, roommate-like relationship for almost one year before we parted ways.

As I told you before, I had the unique talent of sniffing out guys who didn't make me feel safe and never truly committed. I held onto them for dear life—the bigger "maybe" I was in their lives, the more I wanted to win their affection and commitment. I was replaying my childhood story where I wanted to convince my parents to stay, but on a gut level I already knew they would leave. On a gut level, I knew LE and I were too different. His insecure attachment and the emotions it triggered in me were way too familiar.

Back to my mom's advice about staying on the sunny side... I was desperately trying to make her understand that I was a bad person and that it was my fault this relationship was about to end. That I must succumb to the darkest pits of my psyche and clean up the emotional mess that LE made sure to emphasize being the reason for his emotional distancing. My mom kept repeating to me to "stay on the sunny side."

Oh, she frustrated me with her positivity.

I felt she didn't understand me. "Can't she see how messed up I am? How much I deserve to suffer for how badly I ruined things with LE? LE told me it was my emotional inadequacy and lack of maturity that made him so distant, so I must change! My mom is just biased." I legitimately hated myself for a few months. I was in a very dark place. It turned out I didn't understand my mom. She was the wise one. Again.

Don't feel sorry for me. I don't. I have an

amazing life, I love most parts of what I do, I love helping you, I love the freedom I forged for myself. I know that without my life lessons I wouldn't be the person I am today. I am grateful for each and every experience because they made me stronger, more independent, and more resilient. I know that I can overcome anything life throws at me—after crying wet a box of Kleenex, of course.

I told you my story to show you you're not alone. We all have our hidden scars. But they don't have to determine our future. We can pivot. We can accept our baggage and choose to live a better life regardless of what we were "predestined to."

Were you betrayed by your loved ones? You're not alone. Did you experience tremendous loss by someone dear's death? You're not alone. Did illness infiltrate your family? You're not alone. Did you lose all your money? You're not alone. Were you misjudged? You're not alone. Were you emotionally abused? You're not alone. Do you want to heal and thrive, not despite of, but because of all these traumas? You're not alone! Hell, no!

Now you know my story—briefly, but with enough detail. You certainly know your story and how much it overlaps with mine. Maybe a lot, maybe not at all. The interesting thing about traumas is that we all have unique experiences but we heal the same way. The rest of this book will be about that healing.

Chapter 2: Uncovering Emotional Immaturity

In October 2018 I bought an audiobook called *Adult Children of Emotionally Immature Parents*. I got this book with the intention to understand and heal my relationship with my parents, which as you could read in the previous chapter, is complicated. I didn't think that I would step on a self-discovery landmine, which ended up changing my self-image and identity.

As I listened to the book, it became crystal clear to me: I'm not that different than my father emotionally. I do the same things that I resent so much in him. The upbringing he gave me left me with emotional immaturity fleas and some blind spots. Well-meaning friends and LE tried to warn me about my character flaws, but you know how these things go—unless you yourself feel the need to change, the feedback of others will largely be interpreted as criticism. Being unable to take criticism and opposing opinions were two of my key immaturity traits. I snapped, defended myself, and felt that the people closest to me actually didn't love me; they wanted to hurt my feelings, and they didn't understand me. Can you relate to this?

I was so afraid of becoming like my father—yet in many ways I acted just like him. I wasn't able to see this when others told me. But when I allowed myself to be self-critical enough and interpret the words of an objective and unrelated source, a book in this case, it was easy to see how I was influenced by some of his traits I generally disliked.

I make this process sound easy—all you need is self-criticism and a book. But that's not true. You also need some guts and the courage to bleed. Reading something like "I don't take a hard look at my role in the problem." and then saying "Yes, that's me. I do that. And I hurt people I love because of that." Well, that's pure heartache and guilt.

It's not your fault how you've been raised. You had no choice in where you were born and how your parents knew to parent. Beating yourself up because of "whys" won't get you anywhere, it just consolidates your victim attitude and you'll keep looking for responsibility elsewhere. As unfair and as harsh as it sounds, it's your responsibility now, as an adult, to heal yourself. When I was in the pity-party zone I often fumed, "Is it not enough that I had less luck with my upbringing, and that I had to suffer through all that crap? Now it's up to me to suffer through the unlearning and re-learning process, too?" The short answer to this question is "Yes." The long answer is "Hell yeah!" There is no other way. The alternative is to not do the work and keep living at the mercy of your emotions and badly programmed behavior patterns.

Again, it's not your fault what happened in your childhood. But it's your responsibility to deal with it.

We have the tendency to think about adults being more mature than their children. That's not always the case. Some parents lack the emotional responsiveness needed to meet their children's emotional needs largely because they themselves never learned how to do it. Multigenerational emotional neglect is very common in families; where parents just aren't around, aren't giving guidance and emotional care and support for their children. Emotional neglect can have long-term negative impacts on our choices when it comes to relationships, partnerships.

The psychology of emotions and emotional intelligence are fairly new fields of study. So is their importance as a developmental aspect. No wonder our grandparents, the children of the Second World War, and our parents didn't know better. Most parents raised their children with the best of their knowledge and intentions. They didn't mean to be emotionally immature, neglecting. Yet like any voluntary or involuntary neglect, emotional neglect leaves scars. We are the lucky and blessed generation who can know and therefore do better.

If we look at dysfunctional families, there is so much going on, and through all that children get neglected in many different ways. Children internalize everything—when things go wrong, there's a defense system activated in the child to blame themselves for the problem. Why don't they blame the primary caregiver? Because in a child's mind, the primary caregiver is the token of survival; the notion that the parent is able to take care of the child gives them the security that they will be fine. Blaming or internalizing that the parent is dysfunctional would threaten their very core belief of being safe. That's not an option. But something's wrong—so someone must be at fault. If it is not the parent, it's them. This internalization of the family dysfunction, however, creates a wounded child.

A dysfunctional family doesn't have to have mental illness, narcissists, addicts, or physical or sexual abusers to create a wounded child. If the family lacks emotional attunement, doesn't validate the child's emotions, doesn't tell them

60

"I love you," it can by itself make the child question, "Am I lovable?" Emotional neglect doesn't show up in rough cases only. Research shows that emotional neglect can lead to just as many issues as more extreme circumstances.

Children don't know how to regulate their feelings, they learn it through co-regulation. They also can't be in tune with their emotions as they are not at that stage of development. They learn to identify and talk about their emotions if the parent reflects those emotions back to them. For example, if the child looks troubled, an observant parent calls out the child: "You look troubled, what's bothering you?" This way the child learns that the mixture of emotions they are expressing is something called troubled. When the child tells the parent the problem, an emotionally mature parent can further identify what exactly the child is feeling and deepen their understanding about that emotion. This is what it means to be in emotional attunement with the child. If a parent sees the kid being troubled but doesn't take the time to talk about it and validate the child's concerns, that emotion goes by without being validated or understood. The child loses the opportunity to zero in on the emotion and learn to express and manage it.

Attuning and talking about—especially negative—emotions is crucial for the child to learn that feeling those emotions is healthy, normal, and everyone has them. With attention and nurturing these emotions are manageable. The child learns this first with parental guidance, but then when they grow up, will be able to do the emotion management for themselves—as they learned from their parent. Having emotional dialogues early on is needed to grow into emotionally mature adults. The lack of it can leave a child thinking "Am I lovable?" or "Am I worthy? Normal? Adequate? Do my emotions matter?" People who never learned that feeling anger, envy, or sadness is normal, will feel shame or a deep sense of inadequacy when they feel it. They also won't be able to manage it, so they overcompensate with defense mechanisms to make the uncomfortable emotion go away. We'll learn about these defense mechanisms later in this book.

Here are some stories from my readers.

> "I was a surprise child, eight years younger than my next older sibling. I was loved to pieces and cared for very devotedly by my entire family. However, because of the age difference and my siblings finishing their high school years away from home, I became an "only child" by the time I was about

9. At that same time, my parents had a conflict between them that started a cold war that lasted well into my adult years. In addition to my own confusion about the conflict (I did not learn the details until many years later as an adult), I often took on the role of mediator or conciliator. That is not a healthy way for a child to grow up.

The essence of my trial was profound loneliness and a struggle to make things right, over which I had no real control. In the things that meant most to me as a person, I labeled myself a failure. I proceeded to accept positions in life that reinforced that label rather than setting boundaries to protect those parts of who I am that are most dear. I still deal with the consequences of unhealthy coping mechanisms. I still choose unhealthy coping mechanisms when I know better." L. G. C.

"I am a middle age African—born and bred in Africa. My upbringing was a disaster. I was not allowed to express myself freely, I was not supposed to ask questions of my parents or elders; beating was common, happening so much that every little breach of rule called for a beating. As I was growing up I developed a negative approach to everything I did or tried to do. This affected me to the extent that I could not decide on the course my life should take—I easily accepted what others suggested and nothing could come from me." J. K.

"I lived through two decades of family rejection from affection, positive attention, recognition, and I was put down in mean ways and told I'm not one of them (a member of the family I was blood related to) because I was half white instead of half not-white. My family is mixed in ethnicity. The same happened at school as well because I didn't relate well to my white classmates. I found I was good academically and athletically and that carried me until I wasn't allowed to play sports in high school because the family leader made up stories that my mother believed and so I was punished/disciplined through taking away sports. It was downhill from there, and although I've been able to maneuver into a decent career, it isn't sustainable because I'm still struggling with identity, worth, boundaries, and personal discipline because I'm tired of trying and being rejected. One belief that developed is that no matter what I do I won't be accepted/valued, so why push myself to comply with expectations that are hard for me?" E. S.

L. G. C. had to grow up early and act as an adult in his family, being the peacemaker between his parents. That is a burden on a child that he shouldn't carry. J. K. went through a severe repression of identity development paired with physical abuse in a hierarchical family system. E. S. had a similar experience as J. K., facing constant identity crises in a mixed family which also controlled her choices, messing with her sense of individuality. These readers were born and raised on different continents, had different family structures, various level of wealth, yet the emotional outcomes of their childhood experiences are eerily similar.

Those who grew up in homes where one or both parents were emotionally immature experience a deep sense of emotional loneliness. This feeling comes from never being totally considered, valued, and nourished emotionally as a child.[i] This is not to say emotionally immature parents are completely inadequate to care for their children. Quite the contrary, they are very often totally normal parents who deeply engage in the child's physical wellbeing and safety. They work long hours to keep the family afloat and provide the best way they can with the best of intentions. Yet, for the child, emotional neglect can result in feelings of loneliness and insecurity.

Emotional loneliness doesn't show on the outside and its negative impacts affect us negatively only later in life. Some refer to this state as "being alone in the world." It makes sense, as these adult children felt somewhat alone from the very beginning—even when a caretaker was around.

Let's take a trip back to your childhood. Imagine the following two scenarios.

One: You and your preschool friend got into a fight over a toy. You went home and complained about the incident to your parents. They were watching TV so they responded slightly irritated, saying something in a hurry about the value of sharing and that you were an envious little soul and that next time you should share the toy. You went to bed feeling unheard, scolded, and ashamed. You felt unprotected by your parents and utterly alone. Next time you had a conflict with other kids you didn't share it with your parents, and so the feeling of being alone and having no one to count on just grew in your heart.

Two: You and your little preschool friend got into a fight over a toy. You went home and complained about the incident to your parents. They were watching TV but once they heard the sorrow in your voice, they turned it off and invited you to the couch with them. They asked a couple questions about the incident trying to make sense of the situation and giving you the impression that they genuinely cared. They asked you why you felt like not sharing the toy. You confessed that you were afraid the toy would love the other little boy more than it loves you. Your parents validated your fear of losing love with a smile and then they explained that the wonder of love is that it grows once it is shared. It just multiplies, never decreases, so you shouldn't fear because your toy will only love you more for helping it love other kids, too. There is a great value in sharing, as it creates even more love. You understood the example and went to bed happy for being listened to, and looking forward to the next day to share your toy with your friend to generate even more love.

Can you see the difference in the two stories? We are talking about the same event and the same moral, yet the first story comes from a place of emotional immaturity and the second from emotional maturity. Children who experience the first scenario will be encouraged to hide, lie, and share less in the future as honesty got them in trouble. Those who go through the second scenario will feel heard and loved, and will internalize the lesson as well. They will deepen the bond with their parents.

Life is not so black and white. Even the most emotionally mature people snap and make mistakes once in a while when they are tired, overwhelmed, or otherwise distracted. If you just recognized yourself, "Oh dear, I did that first story just the other day!" don't be too hard on yourself. We make mistakes. What matters is that we recognize that we were not too loving and mature and we correct our shortcoming readily and swiftly.

All of us swing on the axis of emotional maturity and immaturity. The extreme of either condition is almost inexistent. Very few people are completely immature adults who act the worst way possible every single time. The same stands true for maturity; we won't act in a mature way 100% of the time, but we can do our best and try.

Signs of Emotional Immaturity

Emotionally immature parents struggle to express genuine emotions. Emotional closeness often makes them withdraw as they can't handle it. They are not self-reflective. When it comes to facing reality they often use defense mechanisms to resist it. They avoid taking responsibility, accepting blame, or apologizing. There is a constant inconsistency between their words and actions, which makes them unreliable. Their problems usually prevail compared to those of their children—the needs of whom they're often unaware.

As a child you can't identify your parent's emotional immaturity, or that your emotional needs are not met properly. You can't conceive notions abstract as these at a young age. All you know is the gut-level feeling of emptiness. Children are reactive little creatures. When they feel hunger, they cry. When they are tired, they cry. And when they feel emotionally needy, they go to the parent for comfort. When the parent fears emotional closeness, their reaction to the child's request for emotional bonding won't be satisfactory, as we saw in that first story before.

Children may carry this sense of emptiness into their adulthood, subconsciously repeating the patterns learned in their childhood. They may choose friends and partners who are emotionally unresponsive, thus they continue being followed by this sense of emotional isolation. The cycle gets reinforced. Getting familiar with the concept of emotional immaturity will shed light on why you felt so lonely as a child, even when your parents were assuring you about their love. Self-awareness and knowledge can help you break the cycle.

My wish for you is that by reading this book you'll gain understanding and an explanation why interactions with some of your family members or closest friends were so painful, why they left you depleted and emotionally dry. Once you gain that clarity, you'll be able to be less frustrated about their behavior, and also less critical about your own likeability.

The bad news is that while you're getting familiar with the concept of emotional immaturity, the immature person will not change. On the bright side, you'll gain awareness about who your loved ones are and you can adjust your expectations regarding the closeness you two can create. You'll be able to detach from the pain their lack of emotional closeness causes you by understanding that they are not capable of more with their current knowledge. It's not your fault, or inadequacy, that your mother or father didn't show you more affection and care. Their neglect was not about you, but about them. Emotionally disengaging from such parents is the path to build or restore self-sufficiency, self-esteem, and self-trust.

The behavior of your parents or close loved ones will make much more sense once you look at it through the lens of emotional immaturity.

We need to understand, as a first step, what we're dealing with. Let me list some signs of emotional immaturity. Do you recognize your parents, other loved ones, or yourself in them?

- They often overreact to relatively small problems;
- They don't express a lot of empathy or emotional awareness;
- They feel uncomfortable when it comes to emotional closeness;
- They are often irritated by others' different points of view or differences;
- They sometimes use people as confidants but they are not a good listener in return;

- They are often inconsistent with their reactions. Sometimes they can react harshly, sometimes calmly to the same situation;
- If someone requires their advice on an emotional problem, they either give a superficial answer or become bothered;
- They cannot truly empathize;
- Even minor disagreements or criticism can make them very defensive;
- They often argue based on what they feel, not based on facts and logic;
- They are seldom self-reflective;
- They have a victim attitude;
- They don't look for their role in a problem; and
- They feel discomfort when asked to be more open-minded, receptive to new ideas or experiences.[ii]

How many of these sentences describe the behavior of your loved one? According to psychologist Lindsay C. Gibson, these are signs of potential emotional immaturity. She highlights that to consider any of the statements relevant, they must happen repeatedly as a behavior pattern to be considered a real warning sign of emotional immaturity.

If you could recognize yourself in these sentences, don't be alarmed. You can build up your emotional maturity from here. I could. The first step is admitting: "Yes, I'm emotionally immature in some aspects." It's hard to nail down our day-to-day emotionally immature reactions as these patterns show up so automatically and unconsciously that you are often unaware of them. If you really want to get to the bottom of the question *"Does this statement apply to me?"* ask three close friends or relatives to share their observations about you in light of the statements above.

Being emotionally immature is not a death sentence. If there is courage of awareness and a willingness to change, these traits can mature, so to speak. Without these two key factors, however, the chances that an emotionally immature person will change—for the better—are slim. If you identified your loved one as such, reading this book you'll understand why they have obstacles to loving kindly. Once you understand this, you may be able to make an informed decision on the kind of relationship you want to have with them in the future. This realization will help you return your focus to yourself as you'll see there's nothing you can do for your emotionally immature parent. It has to be their awareness, their commitment, and their hard work to change themselves.

Am I Being Wounded?

Asking this question is a great start. It means that you may have tapped into a part of yourself that needs healing. Taking a look at your relationships is always a good place to begin your self-reflection. Looking at all sort of relationships in your life can provide you valuable feedback on where you need healing; it could affect friendships, work relationships, intimate partners, family ties. If you have a history of a lot of drama, like very intense romantic relationships, or the absence of it; a lot of arguments with friends where you lose them or you cut each other off; you can't keep a job for long—these are all signs of something going on under the surface. If you can identify any kind of similar pattern in your life it may be a good time to stop and get curious about it. These patterns may arise from your wounded child, which still holds a lot of power over your actions and how you relate to people. Ask: "What am I doing? Where is this pattern coming from? What emotions lead my actions?"

If you honestly answer these questions, most probably you'll tap into some defense mechanisms you developed in your childhood to protect yourself from emotional neglect, abuse, or other forms of deprivation. In the next chapter I will talk about some of the most common defense mechanisms in detail.

Chapter 3: Defense Mechanisms

In this chapter I'd like to talk about our natural defense mechanisms. Everybody has a defense mechanism that they use to protect themselves from emotional pain. A defense mechanism is something that people use to put a wall up between the outside world and their true and honest feelings. Understanding our defenses intimately is the key to reconnecting with ourselves and others, and is also an important step in being able to get rid of them.

When we look at defenses, we can put them in two boxes: there are the defenses of perception—how we perceive things growing up—and there are defensive behaviors. They can be at work at the same time.

Being stoic and emotionless is a defense mechanism. So is smiling when you are talking about something sad or painful—people feel embarrassed and try to mask this emotion with smiling. Being snappy and unwilling to listen is another form of defense mechanism. Disassociating from your emotions as well. As is rationalizing. These defenses are really tools to disconnect you from your true, emotional self. To become emotionally mature, you need to keep these defenses in check and become capable of grappling with uncomfortable emotions.

The Origins of Defense Mechanisms

A little psychoanalytic theory… defense mechanisms are strategies of our unconscious mind to manipulate, deny, or distort reality, and defend against feelings of anxiety and unacceptable impulses to maintain our personal mental frameworks, otherwise known as schemas.[iii] The term defense mechanism was first coined by Sigmund Freud in 1894. He compartmentalized a person's psyche's structure into three parts:

- The Id, the unconscious, the libido, the psychic energy that empowers instincts and psychic processes. It is a selfish, childish, pleasure-oriented part of the personality with no ability to delay gratification.
- The Superego, responsible for our internalized cultural and moral codes learned from parents and society. The Superego distinguishes "good" from "bad," "right" from "wrong."
- The Ego is the moderator between the pleasure seeker id and the moralistic

superego, looking for compromises to pacify both.[iv]

The ego uses defense mechanisms to protect us from feeling anxious or guilty, states that arise from id or superego demands. These defenses operate at an unconscious level and they are normal to have. They can, however, get out of proportion if used regularly, leading to neuroses such as chronic anxiety, obsessive behavior, phobias, or hysteria.[v]

Defense mechanisms are similar to the soft spots we've discussed, in that they are part of a person's psychological make-up—they are there for a reason, and when an intimate partner or a person close to us pokes at them or judges them, it hurts. A lot.

Defense mechanisms are not ideal behavior, especially in an attempt to be intimately close to someone. But they are also not malicious or used with bad intention. They are a way of distancing oneself from the truth of something so that the pain is more tolerable. Personal growth and emotional development lead to lowering one's defense mechanisms, particularly when interacting with someone close to their heart. Instead of covering up the authentic truth with certain self-protective behaviors, the truth should be shared in a genuine and honest and vulnerable way.

When someone arrives at a high level of self-awareness, they are surprised to find out that defenses have a higher pain cost than vulnerability. This discovery says a lot about the path of one's life and personal growth; there once was a time in the life of that person when the defenses were more important than anything else. That's exactly why they were created in the first place. But as with most grown adults, one reaches a point in life and in emotional development where the defenses no longer serve them as they did when they were first constructed. Not only are they not serving them, they are actually harming them.

It's a good place to be where you say you don't need your old defenses—that they are no longer serving you the way they used to—so you need to peel them off and move on. Then you arrive to a point where you open your life and heart to better things.

Common Types of Defense Mechanisms

1. Morphing

I learned early in life how to please people and get my way. I was practicing this skill on my dad, persuading him to buy me things by becoming the little girl I knew he wanted me to be. I went fishing with him, I played a laid-back character (just as he pretended to be), I started telling him stories (lies) of being a tiny female Casanova because that was the image he was projecting about himself, and I generally agreed with him in everything. Later, I applied this same strategy with people I needed help from. I became whoever they wanted me to be.

The healthy version of morphing is mirroring; the latter is the good intention of building rapport by copying the body language, mood, and talking style of another person. Morphing is different. I felt a bit like being an empty canvas and only adopted a personality when I was the reflection of someone else. Yes. It's a tough way of being, and it's even tougher when after 27 years you realize that you've been doing it and you pose yourself the question: Who am I? What do I actually like? What do I actually want? I struggled with these questions for months until I finally had the clarity and courage to pin them down. It's a scary thing to state out loud: this is who I am and this is what I like, knowing that for some you'll be unlikable. Being unlikable is a people pleaser's greatest fear, after all.

That being said, morphing is not the worst defense mechanism to have if you can use it well and, in congruence with your authentic self, tuning it down to mirroring. People do like to see themselves reflected in another person. They may feel more at ease, understood, and cared for, which are fundamental wants of human nature and they go back to very early childhood. Narcissistic and self-absorbed people can't get enough of themselves being reflected back. For other people, it's a welcomed thing too, because most people never got enough validation from their primary caregivers in childhood. If you offer this to a person, they're going to like you. And if you use this skill with good intention, that creates a win-win situation. Your morphing/mirroring can become of value and help other people emotionally in ways that they don't even realize. Morphing in this sense is indeed a good survival mechanism. And it can be a tool of offering genuine empathy and understanding to others.

Should you unlearn morphing if you identified it as a defense mechanism you use? I would say, not necessarily. At a certain stage of awareness, I think it's more important to understand why you do your morphing. Get a good grasp on what it is and why it is happening. And when it's happening—or better yet, understanding when you have the urge to do it (before you've done it, preferably). Ideally, before considering unlearning or eradicating it, you want to really get close with it, and know it, closely. Beyond knowing it you want to be able to control it. Here I mean consciously choosing whether or not to do it.

Observe yourself and your emotions so that you catch morphing when it's happening, and make a deliberate choice about how much of it you want to do—or even if you want to do it at all. If you can get to that level of consciousness about morphing, you will be in a place where you can embrace it rather than fight it.

2. Defensiveness

Getting defensive once in a while is normal. But notoriously defensive people are hard to take. A person who takes responsibility for their defensiveness is not hard to take at all. It's actually a very admirable and relatable quality, to own something, and to catch it in oneself, then to reel it in. Most people respect those who can do that—own their neuroses, so to speak.

If in your childhood and recent experiences you spent a lot of time buying into the belief that you are inherently flawed as a human being, defensiveness may work on a powerful level in your psyche. Someone making you feel flawed by default as a human being, actually, is one of the worst kinds of emotional abuse. If you've been through such treatment often, you need to do some unlearning.

Intellectually you may already be aware that you are good enough and loveable for who you are. But the old programming running in your mind's background may be telling you otherwise. This is what pushes you to want to defend yourself against things that are not meant to be an attack or offense. There is some rewiring that needs to be done; some reprogramming of an old, destructive message that you are living with. This may take practice and time.

What can you do to rid yourself of your gut reaction to react defensively?

The best thing to do if you catch yourself being defensive is to own it. You can add something like, "Oh, sorry… I feel like I was getting a little defensive there… I didn't mean to. Anyway, [then say something nice to lighten the mood and get back on track with positivity]."

Owning it means just declaring "I was defensive." in a nonchalant way. Like it's no big deal for you to admit it and move on from it. "Sorry, I think I got a little defensive there for a moment…" is better than saying nothing or denying it. The first one is taking full ownership, the second one is escaping responsibility, shifting the burden onto the other person to deal with the emotions you can't or to eat up your dishonesty. But it's not up to the other person to do either of these. It's up to you to declare it, take responsibility for it, and accept, love, and embrace yourself regardless.

Being defensive is something that most people wrestle with throughout their lives. By consciously working on noticing it, you are getting closer to handle it. Every time you catch yourself getting defensive is a chance to then become less defensive going forward. Because each moment you notice it highlights that the old programming is no longer true.

3. Projection

Projection is a funny defense mechanism. It works this way: you take an emotional experience that belongs to you, and you attribute it to another person. It happens with anger all the time. One could be feeling angry at someone, and all of a sudden, one is thinking "They are angry at me!" when that's actually not true. When you're feeling anger, based on your upbringing you may think "But anger is unacceptable, is bad, it makes me a bad person." so you solve this problem by convincing yourself they are angry with you.

When projection is happening, the goal is to own it, and say "That's my stuff." and then take back the projection. Owning it also means being okay with the fact that you have that feeling, rather than feeling anxious about it.

And as long as you don't know for sure what someone's thinking and feeling you can't act and judge as if you would know. Stop and take a hard look at your assumptions. It's tempting to look at someone's actions and ascribe meaning to them—especially because you are trying to protect yourself from pain. It's also tempting to look at another person's behavior and say to yourself what you'd feel and do if you did what that person is doing. For example, you started dating a new guy and he is a bit slow at responding to your messages. You might think, "If I was treating someone this unresponsive way, it would mean that I am not that into them. Therefore, the fact that he is treating me this way must also mean that he is just not that into me." But projection is ascribing your way of being onto someone else. The truth is, more information is needed—from the person himself.

In the absence of information about whether you are being wanted, valued, appreciated, and so on, there is anxiety. There is the fear that you are losing ground. Without confirmation of the things you need, it's easy to jump to conclusions, to say "This is bad!" and run with anxiety as the conclusion.

You spin yourself into a self-made drama, which, in this case, is not knowing why the guy is unresponsive. When you defend yourself with projection to get rid of anxiety, what you really want is a sense of security. The question is, can you get it? Can you have the kinds of conversations with the guy—at the right time and place—that lead you both to some good communication, and provide for you with the information you need?

Ask honest questions to discover what you need to know. Fill in the gaps in your mind with genuine information from the source instead of anxiety and projection. You'll want to practice asking questions that sound authentic, pure, gentle, even vulnerable, and with childlike curiosity as opposed to questions that sound like an interrogation loaded with hidden intentions. You want to be able to ask genuine questions about how someone thinks and feels (about you) without them ever feeling suspicious of why you are asking.

Such questions may start like this:

- "I'm wondering…"
- "I would like to understand better…"
- "What do you mean by…"

4. Rationalizing

Do you stay in relationships where you are not appreciated and loved the way that's fulfilling to you? Do you explain it with things like "That's just how men are." or "That's how long-term relationships go"? Do you keep being friends with people who are not kind to you and don't show up in times of need, saying "Oh well, that's just how things are"?

This would be the defense mechanism of rationalizing at play: a cognitive distortion of facts to make them less threatening. When things go wrong we look for ways to rationalize them: "It happened because of this…" We do this quite often on a fairly conscious level. We may do it so often that some of our excuses may become our reality; we end up believing our own lies, in other words.

Look for behavior patterns rather than individual events when you diagnose yourself as a chronic rationalizer. If you rationalize the behavior of someone (or your own) only once in a while, you may just genuinely try to give people the benefit of the doubt, which is a good trait to have. But if you constantly rationalize the hurt other people cause you—or you to others—tolerating the pain without setting boundaries might mean that you are defending yourself against a greater pain, like the fear of abandonment, being inadequate, or being judged. The level of pain you associate with losing a person seems greater, more threatening, than rationalizing away the sting this person's judgment, let's say, caused in you.

Rationalization often takes the form of comparison. For example, "Yes, I did that… but the neighbor did something ten times worse." Or "My partner often ignores me, but the partner of my best friend cheated, so…" This defense mechanism can also get us to avoid admitting disappointment: "I didn't get the job but I wasn't so thrilled about it in the first place…" Or a mixture of avoiding disappointment and comparison: "Yes, but being an (undesired job) is better than an (even more repelling job)."

On the bright side, rationalization can reduce the discomfort caused to people by cognitive dissonance, awareness of their inconsistent thinking patterns. [vi] On the down side, rationalization can make us seem dishonest and keep us in situations that actively harm us—or others. We can rationalize ourselves deeply into self-sabotage.

Do you have a high tolerance for pain (emotional, psychological, or even physical)? Do you tend to minimize things? Do you intellectualize everything and totally disconnect from your emotions?

Then it's time to do something about it. I don't know about you, but to me the most frequent rationalization-triggering emotions are guilt and shame. When I know I'm doing something contrary to my values like procrastinating, giving in to Nutella, or skipping the gym, I tend to rationalize out of guilt. When I feel like I'm not doing enough to start something, or I'm looked down upon, my rationalizing is triggered by shame.

It's a good thing to become aware of our habits. Just on the level I wrote about them above. When you do so and so, it's because of this or that emotion. This kind of awareness can make all the difference when you're challenged by rationalization. Once you nail down the pattern, you can ask yourself why you do what you do.

Step 1: What is the action (or lack of it) that triggers rationalization?
Step 2: What emotion is behind the rationalization of the (in)action?

Step 3: Why do you use rationalization as a defense?

The answer to Step 3 is usually the defense mechanism's origin story. For example, when I feel guilty because I procrastinated, that's usually because of my grandmother, who couldn't sit still and whoever did nothing was labeled lazy and unworthy in her eyes. So when I do nothing I tend to think of myself as a lazy, unworthy person, which is painful. So I start rationalizing. "I only procrastinate now because…I'm sick/I don't have time to finish my task anyway so why even start/I have other things to do, etc."

Why is it important to know all this? Because from here I can pivot. I need to do something about my bad habit of procrastination, that's true, but doing something for the sake of not disappointing my dead grandmother is not the best reason. Doing something about the choking guilt behind my defense mechanism, however, is a good idea. As an adult I can see my grandmother's shortcomings, too. How impatient she was, and how desperately she tried to avoid something by not staying put for ten seconds. It was her issue, her agenda, whatever she was fighting with. Her poor opinion on procrastination doesn't make anyone a bad person for procrastinating. Sometimes only making this cause-effect connection between pain and its origin story can be enough to break out of the unhealthy pattern.

Generally speaking, the antidote of rationalization is actual logic—but logic that takes soft variables like emotions into consideration. Emotions do make sense, we just need to find where they are coming from.

Chapter 4: On Boundaries

Have you ever felt like your gut pushed you to say something, do something, stand up for yourself, and... you just couldn't? I felt that way awfully often in the past.

Here is one example. LE loved to play rough. He was not aggressive or violent per se, but he liked to wrestle me into submission. I'm not talking about anything kinky here, only the simple childish bravado fights that end with one party crying. That party was usually me. I didn't cry literally, only on the inside. I so disliked being treated like some mischievous little brother who gets dominated by his big brother twice his size. I often ended up with blue and green bruises, bite marks, and a devastated soul of not having my feminine fragility considered at all.

I wasn't totally innocent in the matter, though, for two reasons. Having the spirit I have, I never backed off and I resisted the siege valiantly hoping that I may win this fight. I only let LE know he hurt me when… well, when it hurt so much I couldn't hide it. The other reason that made me responsible for this situation was my lack of boundaries around the issue. I didn't stand up for myself, to kindly but firmly tell LE I didn't like playing rough and that my preference was to be considered a dainty princess, not a little boy. I didn't do it. Why?

Because, just like you when you stay silent without boundaries, I was afraid. I feared that if I spoke up, I'd lose LE's interest. I'd lose his love and I'd distance him. I rather forced myself mentally to be okay with the beastly plays on a regular basis. Even though whenever the thought "Could you live with this for your whole life?" creeped inside my head, a voice deep down desperately yelled, "No! Hell no!"

I didn't listen to that voice deep down. I didn't dare listen, as I learned that what I wanted rarely mattered. That I had no control over my life anyway—it doesn't matter what I do. That I needed LE to survive. It was an absolutely irrational fear, for sure, but in those times of hardship it caused me severe anxiety attacks.

Many of us who were brought up in dysfunctional families—be it dysfunctional because of substance abuse, mental health conditions, narcissism, or simply knowing no better—and had toxic relationships may suffer of the following things: codependency and learned helplessness.

Codependency is a behavioral condition in a relationship where one person enables another person's addiction, poor mental health, immaturity, irresponsibility, or underachievement. The main characteristics of codependency include excessive reliance on other people for approval and a sense of identity. [vii] Karen Horney, a German psychologist, was the first who mentioned the idea of what we call codependency today in 1941. She stated that some people are prone to adopt a "Moving Towards" personality style to escape their anxiety; they move toward others by seeking their approval and affection, and subconsciously control them through their dependent style. A person suffering from codependency is usually "unselfish, virtuous, martyr-like, faithful, and turns the other cheek despite personal humiliation."[viii]

Learned helplessness is a coping mechanism that can be adopted in our family of origin, or even later in life, because of a dysfunctional relationship. Being traumatized and abused as a young child can lead to learned helplessness. Even smaller dysfunctions can leave their mark on us. If our parents were notoriously worried and saw the world as a dangerous place, we might adopt a similar worldview. If our parents were generally optimistic and had a positive outlook on life, we may become just the same. Learned helplessness is the perception of the absence of control over the outcome of a situation. One is convinced that life just happens to them and there is nothing they can do to influence their life, thus they choose to do nothing. Who was taught that life just happens to them was taught to be helpless. This, of course, is inaccurate—there are many areas of our lives we have control over, but if we believe we don't, then we don't. We can't change our lives for the better unless we feel empowered enough to do so. And we can't feel empowered if we don't start to believe that life can get better for us. The good news is, as the name of the condition suggests, this kind of helplessness is learned. Thus you can unlearn this conditioning.

How do you overcome codependency and learned helplessness? Codependency and learned helplessness is an insidious combo of self-sabotaging habits. We feel the need to please others and we also believe there's nothing we can do differently. As with everything, we start by becoming aware of our behavior patterns. What are yours? Do you please people out of fear of… (loss, abandonment, being worthless, etc.)? Do you think that your life can't be changed, you can't be helped, or you can't do anything differently? When do you have these thoughts? What events trigger them? Who triggers them? When was the first time you felt genuinely helpless? What age? Can you answer these questions? If so, write them down. We need to map out your codependency-learned helplessness patters so we can do something about them. Because we, *you*, can do something about them.

After becoming intimate about what you do and why, the next step towards change is setting appropriate boundaries to create some space for yourself to heal. This means cutting out or distancing yourself from people who make you feel helpless, codependent, or both.

When we behave in a codependent and/or helpless way, we lack two things: on one hand, we didn't learn how to draw healthy boundaries as our parents weren't good examples for us, and on the other hand, even if we had the inclination to protect our boundaries, we don't know how to verbalize our request for keeping our boundaries.

For me it was a tricky road to develop both skills. Whenever I felt that I was ready to protect myself—so to say—whatever left my mouth was rather a rude, defensive course of sentences. I had no idea how to defend my boundaries and stay respectful of the other person at the same time. I had no idea of concepts such as "taking things personally" or "he didn't mean to hurt you." I took everything very personally, and the critical things others said were like an arrow directed towards my heart with the explicit intent to crush it. There was a time when I was convinced the world revolved around me and everyone and everything was out to get me. So I needed to be vigilant and ready to fight. But at the same time I was terrified of losing people like LE, so I kept my silence just as often as I erupted in a snappy outburst. Long story short, I didn't understand my emotions, and I wasn't in control of them. I was mostly reactive.

Fixing our boundary issues is step two. Step one has to be self-understanding. Getting familiar with our emotions and behavior patterns, why we feel some things—it's useful to dig out where those emotions are coming from, and most importantly how we want to handle them.

Being in control of our reactions (we can hardly control our emotions) gives us a sense of self-trust and self-empowerment. I was afraid to protect my boundaries for the following reasons:

- I didn't consider myself important enough to speak up.

- I felt that if I lost someone important by speaking up, my world would end.
- I didn't know how to articulate my boundary issues respectfully—I was afraid of my own self.
- I feared criticism even if I nailed my defense speech.

In LE's case, criticism followed in the beginning of our relationship, when I was braver in marking my comfort zone. "You are such a pussy." "You're not fun." "Will you give up so easily?" Adding in the mixture more general criticisms he flashed my way, such as "You're not challenging enough. You don't make me a better person." I was really afraid to disappoint him with one more thing.

In the grand scheme of boundary violations, rough play, of course, is a minor one. But chances are, if we fear making our voice heard on small issues, we will be less likely to do it on big ones.

Take cheating for example. Many of us do stand up at such a grave violation of trust as infidelity, and leave. Others—both parties—get down on their knees proverbially and sometimes literally, and cry, fight, therapy it out, and they come out the other end as a stronger, more unified couple than before. These stories really lift my heart. But there is another group, those who get stuck in between the previous two stages—who are not ready, willing, mature, or forgiving enough to stay, but they also can't leave. They are stuck in this loop of rage, disappointment, self-righteousness, and (often toxic) love. They are the group who are stuck in emotional misery which is leading nowhere. I was stuck in such a situation. Twice.

I always considered infidelity a betrayal, as being a hard, red boundary for me. Whenever I started a relationship with someone, I proudly exclaimed that if he cheats, I'm out. Yet it happened two times with two different men, and I didn't keep my word to myself. My most painful boundary had been destroyed twice, and my psyche went berserk. I loved both men dearly and I didn't want to lose them. But at the same time I wasn't mature enough to get over the offense and work it out together. Neither were they. So we just spiraled down in this vicious cycle of victim-perpetrator.

I felt terrible about the infidelity, sure. But I felt even worse about something that I realized only much later. I was not only betrayed by my partner, but a betrayal of myself took place as well. I betrayed my own boundaries. Back then my focus went onto LE and his actions, and how painful it felt to be on the receiving end of that kind of relationship betrayal. But the deeper betrayal was that I betrayed myself according to something of my own description.

Have you ever felt this way? Not necessarily in the case of infidelity, but any other occasion—when you knew you weren't taking action in accordance with your deepest values. How did you feel afterwards? Did you take responsibility for your choice of actions? Or did you blame the one who caused you pain even more?

There is no wrong answer here, as long as it's honest. I was a huge responsibility avoider and casting the blame on LE gave me peace on the very short term. But blaming him caused a cognitive dissonance in my head, as I wanted to love him. Yet I couldn't because he hurt me. So the only way to make peace in my head was to try to hate him by constantly reminding myself of what he did. This, of course, was not fair to him. I decided to stay and try to forgive him. I did a poor job with that.

Another really important thing I was missing was the cognitive dissonance I created in my head about myself. I told myself that if I ever get cheated on again, I'd pull out—yet I didn't. As far as my right mind was concerned, I was a liar and a self-betrayer. And as much as I wanted to rationalize why I chose to stay with LE, I should have just made peace with the fact that I betrayed my boundaries.

So if you have ever found yourself in a similar situation, here is my take on it. Make order in your own heart and head first. Make peace with your choice. Find forgiveness for what you did to yourself first and foremost. Then use this experience as something to find empowerment from so that you honor your most deeply held boundaries going forward.

We are the watch of our own boundaries. It's up to each one of us to know our boundaries and honor and respect them ourselves first, so that we can share them with others, second.

My boundaries about infidelity or my dad's disingenuous behavior are clear. Those boundaries were born out of adversity, where the emotional pain was intolerable, and today I'm powerful enough to exclaim: enough is enough; I don't want to deal with this anymore! I gained clarity about why I felt so miserable before.

But the most important part of the clarity about these boundaries is the commitment you make to yourself. Since you can never control the actions of another person, having firm boundaries around issues like infidelity, finances, ways you allow yourself to be treated, is not a guarantee that these things won't occur in your life again. But what you do want to guarantee is the commitment to yourself that you will always take care of yourself if ever faced with these situations.

Imagine yourself as a loving adult talking to your young child. You would say something like:

"*I promise you, I will always be there for you and look out for you. I will make sure that you are safe, and I will not stand by and do nothing if bad things are happening to you. I will protect you, and I will move you away from this pain to a better place. I will get you away from this.*"

And then, to uphold the boundary, you must adhere to your promise, and remove yourself from the painful situation.

That is how we exert our boundaries when things are hurting us emotionally. We don't lean in to the pain, but rather, we take the path of least resistance, and separate ourselves from the energy of the harmful circumstance. That is how boundaries are enforced. It's not in what you say to someone, like, "Stop it, you're crossing my boundaries!" But rather, it's what you do with your focus and your energy. You take your attention off the harmful person/location/event, and you focus your attention on restoring your emotional balance. And that is why we say boundaries are about you, not so much the other person.

Boundaries and Personal Energy

In some cases, the need for a boundary is very clear. Such cases are rough play, infidelity, getting financially abused by your parents, but there are much more insidious events that beg for a boundary in your life. They are passive power-draining mechanisms.

For example, there was a time that any time I went home to visit my parents, I felt so drained emotionally and physically by the experience that I felt I wanted to run away. And after a couple of days I just adjusted my personal resonance to this new, lower level of energy and emotional strength. Needless to say, I was much more irritable, less productive, and not the best version of myself overall.

Ever since I had my talk with my parents about my grievances and we could moderately settle our issues, I feel less drained when I visit them. But to achieve this, I needed the talk, and to recognize another boundary I needed to assert, and developing the boundary of my personal energy.

Are you familiar with the term "energy vampires"? They are people who suck life out of you whenever you meet them. Conventionally, we think about this one negative person in our distant friend circle. But we fail to properly consider the nature of vampirism: that no one is born to be a vampire and that some people transform into vampires. My parents weren't always energy vampires, they turned into them as a consequence of lots of unhealed emotional trauma gathered over the years. So did LE. He filled me with loving, positive energy in the beginning of our relationship, and then he slowly turned into someone whom I constantly felt anxious and uncertain around, and these emotions drained me of energy.

Noticing the subtle and not so subtle changes in our energy levels is an important aspect of self-knowledge and self-care. It's up to us to find out what works and what doesn't work for us. Who are the people who decrease our energy and why? Name the people, name the reasons. This awareness is crucial to be able to scoop ourselves out from the damaging dynamic. Then find your personal answer to the following questions:

- Ask yourself, how low are you willing to let your energy go?
- How depleted are you allowed to get?
- How much effort do you want to put in to restoring your energy?
- And preserving it, when it's good?

This practice helps you discover the big picture concept about how you want your life to be. Your emotional energy—whether it's depleted or restored—plays a big role in the quality of your life. So the boundary here is like a car's gas tank. Visualize a gas tank that is full. That's your ideal. That's when you are in alignment with yourself, your anxiety and fear is at a minimum. That's when you live with a certain confidence that you are a trusted watcher of your own boundaries and that you will maintain your personal responsibility to take care of your emotional needs.

Conflicted relationships and negative emotions can cause that gas tank to run out. Are there any alarms set on that tank? Any warnings for you to change what you're doing—what you're allowing into your life?

My therapist, Michelle, said that the notion of making peace with having betrayed one's own boundaries has to do with the promise and the commitment one makes to oneself about how they're going to handle boundary-breaking circumstances in the future. It also has to do with admitting to yourself that when you allowed your own personal boundaries to be broken, and as a result—suffered a lot of emotional pain—you dropped the ball on your own self care. That's when one has a talk with oneself and says, "*Self, I messed up; I let you down. I'm going to look after you better, going forward; I promise!*" And then, your same self responds by saying back, "*Thank you; I appreciate that; I forgive you for making that mistake; I'm glad you've got my back.*"

You Are Entitled to Have Your Boundaries

LE was a highly critical person. He called me on my BS—which was a great gift—in the harshest, coldest way I ever experienced—which was a huge boulder on the great gift. I often became very defensive and deaf to his comments not because of what he said but how he said it.

Can you relate? Has someone dear to you ever criticized you out of love and with the hope to help you, but they did it in such a demeaning way their message never got to you? (And then you also got blamed for being oversensitive, snappy, and unable to receive criticism?)

I'm familiar with this feeling from much earlier than LE. It is in fact a childhood trauma I suffered from my paternal grandparents. I was never good enough—no matter what I did.

Their putdown was swift, cold, and distant, and as a child, living in a very warm and loving environment at my maternal grandparents', this treatment came as a shock. I was afraid and anxious every time I went to my father's parents. When I connected the early-life emotions of feeling inadequate, devalued, unloved, and unworthy with LE's way of dropping criticism, I made a very strong case for why I feel the way I feel today, and why I react the way I react to certain emotionally charged situations—with blame, cold words, and emotional distance. I have proven and legitimized beyond a shadow of a doubt that I am justified in stating:

Because of this negative past experience, I do not—or will not—tolerate any more blame coming in my direction. *"I can't take it anymore. It is a red boundary. Or black. I don't want more of that. I don't want to be blamed anymore.*" I think I said these exact words to my therapist.

What I want to emphasize with regard to any personal boundary is that you are entitled to declare it. And you are entitled to declare such a boundary even *without* any solid, logical explanation I provided. In the beginning of my self-discovery journey I felt that giving a good enough reason why I declare a boundary would work as a safety net. It was a covert defense mechanism on my side to try to tell people, "Look, I know this boundary is annoying for you as you have to change your behavior from now on for us to stay friends, but please don't be angry with me. Here is a list of reasons why I'm asking for what I ask." Can you empathize with the feeling? It's boundary setting lite, where you still want to make sure you'll keep the person in question in your life.

The truth is, those who deeply and honestly care about you won't require you to explain yourself. It is important to them to treat you the best possible way they can. So they will ultimately welcome your cry for a boundary; it's firsthand guidance on how to treat you well.

- If you phrase your need for a boundary the right way to the right people, that's a win-win situation, as you'll get the treatment you want and they will know how to love you better.
- If you state your need for a boundary the right way to the wrong people, that's a win-lose situation where you win by eliminating a person from your life who didn't love you purely in the first place. And it's a lose for them for failing to learn from your example of asserting a boundary, and they also lose

a person who is on their best path for a higher self.
- If you phrase your need for a boundary the wrong way to the right people, you may still be able to pull out a win-win as people who care about you will lovingly tell you that your message made sense but your tone didn't, so you can mutually grow from that situation.
- If you share your need for a boundary the wrong way to the wrong people, you'll get blamed, gaslighted, and probably discouraged in your further attempts to speak up. People like these should be kept at an arm's length, at least.

It is very important to assert your boundaries to the right people first and foremost, and the right way. A good therapist can help you with what language to use. Is your partner mature enough to take such an assertion well? If not, what can you do?

Later in this chapter I will also provide some tips, which you can use to get a head start in the boundary-setting question. But every situation is different, there is no one-size-fits-all advice here, I'm afraid. Before we get to that part, remember this:

You get to determine and uphold your personal boundaries, even without having a case to prove them to others.

If you put a lot of energy into explaining yourself, try to tone it down to just your journal. Validating, legitimizing yourself and your actions, and the emotions that go with them belong to you in most cases. There are cases when and where you need to be explaining or justifying yourself and when you don't—or shouldn't—exert the effort. Sometimes it's okay to just be the way you are, without having to prove or explain why you are the way you are.

How Do You Expand Your Boundaries in a Loving Way?

One important thing to keep in mind: in having strong boundaries one doesn't need to say mean or hurtful things to others. But that doesn't mean that others won't get hurt. Sometimes they will, and that is more a consequence of their own deficiencies or limitations. A good way to express your boundaries goes along these steps:

- Stay away from "you" statements, instead, focus on "I" statements. ("You are too negative." "Because of you I…")

- Speak from your own experience of what you wish, what you need, and what you feel. ("I feel that…" "I need to…" "I wish we could at least…")

Sometimes, people live their life in an emotionally immature way. They need to grow but they're not able to for one reason or another. If you set healthy boundaries for yourself, you are acting as a role model for them, whether they want to see it or not. If they themselves are too caught up in victimhood, they may not want to take responsibility for their own ways, and they may want to shift blame on you by telling you you're mean, or that you don't understand them.

If they choose to do that, that is unfortunate—for them. What matters is that you become okay with this outcome too; not because you prefer it, but because you understand it, and you realize that healthy boundaries (by you or anyone) are more important than emotional lacking and limitation. By setting healthy boundaries for yourself, you may even help someone else wake up.

When we want to set boundaries we often have the desire to want to say, "Please try to avoid doing this or that in the future." It's tempting to want to tell the other person how to behave so that we feel more comfortable. But stating something like that is a form of control.

For example, my new partner called me needy. This is a trigger word for me and I took it very personally. He tried to control the situation to his own comfort when he said, "Don't be needy." That's a bit of a blaming statement; there's no vulnerability or authenticity in it. I could have snapped back and protected my wounded heart saying something like, "Don't call me needy!" This is a similarly insensitive response. Instead, the more empowered and mature way to handle such an experience is to say something about yourself, an "I" statement. Something like, "Needy? I don't like being called that. Why do you think I'm being needy?" This is an authentic reaction, I don't try to play away the fact that his words hurt me but I also don't answer fire with fire. I gave my partner information about a label I dislike, and then took myself out of the hot seat by asking him to explain himself.

It turned out that, to my partner, needy meant something totally different than what it meant to me, so we ended up laughing about it and also got to know each other a bit better. Had I snapped and attacked him for his "insensitivity," I would have built walls, not bridges, between us.

Expressing Boundaries on Jokes

This might be an odd choice of topic but I think many of us struggle to set boundaries when we become the target of innocent but uncomfortable jokes. I don't know about you but I often have the internal struggle when someone hurts me with their joke to either make my pain heard and be a party pooper, or pretend I found the joke funny and boil inside. If you find yourself in this position, don't worry. It's not insane to debate these two possibilities—we'd like to come across as easygoing, likable, and chill in the eyes of our peers. You can assess how intentional, rude, or nasty the joke was. You can choose to let it go if you're aware that the joke itself was not mean, but it touched a sensitive spot in you—but that's not the other person's fault.

However, when the "jokes" are being said at our expense, it's good to let the other person know it. Most people with bad jokes really are not out to harm us, and they might care enough about our well-being to not want to bring us frustration with insensitive remarks. In this case, they need to know they touched a soft spot. "Jokes" about physical violence directed at us—in my case, a joke about pushing me down the stairs if I got pregnant—are just not funny. Even a laidback person should not just settle for that line of thinking. If someone directs that kind of thinking or "joking" your way, you want to stop them in their tracks, saying something like, "Wait... what? Not funny. That's a harsh statement!" It's okay to react to this type of joke. The initiator of the joke—who in most cases is a man, no offense—needs to check himself. Think about the situation in reverse. What if you said that one good way of taking care of birth control would be to cut his balls off in the middle of the night? If you said that and started laughing at your own "joke," he would think you were a little lunatic. Not too many men would laugh along with you. Because it's not funny. Violence is not that funny to grown-ups. If you don't want to sound too rigid in your expression of discomfort a joke has caused you, you can say, "It's only funny when both of us are laughing."

This is a tricky situation in assessing your boundaries, as you want to be perceived as lighthearted but you're getting your feelings hurt in the meantime. However, practicing to be your authentic self requires you to have genuine reactions that express how you truly feel about a situation. It takes practice, and people who care about you may get shocked the first or second time you stand up for yourself, but eventually they will learn how to treat you better.

Chapter 5: Narcissism

The first time I heard of the word narcissism I recalled that little dwarf from the cartoon *Smurfs* who had a flower in his hat and kept kissing his reflection in the mirror. The cartoon's character was sweet and lovable. Real narcissism is not so endearing.

A narcissistic person loves themselves first and foremost. This being said, not every self-centered, know-it-all person is a narcissist. In this chapter we will explore the difference between real narcissists and self-absorbed people. Then we'll talk about fleas. Not the little, annoying black bugs, but character fleas: a term used in psychology for children or partners of people who behave in narcissistic ways or are real narcissists. It turns out some unhealthy behavior patterns can rub off on us temporarily, and just like with real fleas, we need to make sure we get rid of them before we give them to someone else.

I would like to highlight that the information in this chapter can be upsetting, and if you have the tendency to internalize things that apply to you even if just a little bit… don't. Just because you occasionally exhibit traits or behaviors that are the hallmarks of narcissists, it doesn't mean that you're a narcissist. It means that either you have been "infected" with fleas or that—like all of us—you still have room for improvement in your behavior. The greatest sign of you not being a narcissist is becoming worried of being a narcissist. Real narcissists don't worry about that. They would read this chapter and think about some other narcissist in their circle of acquaintances that fits this profile. They wouldn't think this chapter talks about them.

What Are Narcissists Made Of?

Let's define who a true narcissist is. A narcissist is more than your average obnoxious, self-absorbed homo erectus you can't stand. A person who suffers from the clinically diagnosable version of narcissism, otherwise know as Narcissistic Personality Disorder (NPD), is a different piece of cake. This condition affects less than one percent of the total population and the majority of these people are men.[ix] The diagnosis and term of narcissism has been around since 1911 and got included into the Diagnostic and Statistical Manual (DSM) in 1980.[x] Yet not everyone who acts in narcissistic ways is pathological. As you can see, 99% of the population is not a real narcissist. In other words, every narcissist has a

145

narcissistic personality type, but not everyone with a narcissistic personality type is a narcissist.

I feel the need to chew this bone of distinction more. I used to think that just because I hated sharing my food, and yet demanded the food of other people, I was a narcissist. I was just a little brat. But for months I suffered thinking that I was a terrible human being. I don't want you to think that about yourself. Acting in narcissistic ways is part of human evolution, it's a form of survival. "I come first." Yet, if taken to an extreme, it can be considered a maladaptive survival skill, as alienating people from us by acting in selfish, unloving ways is actually dangerous from a survival point of view. If your tribe hated you for being so full of yourself and uncaring about the needs of the tribe, they might let the lion eat you first.

The clinical definition of NPD is "a mental condition in which people have an inflated sense of their own importance, a deep need for excessive attention and admiration, troubled relationships, and a lack of empathy for others."[xi] These people usually have a distorted self-image, are overinvested in themselves, lack empathy, they exaggerate their achievements, they take advantage of others, and they just generally don't care about anything and anyone but themselves. They are not pure evil. They have a complex mental condition that makes life miserable for them, too, not just to those around them. It is a mental illness, not a messed up moral compass.

They need special help. Psychotherapy is the most effective form of treatment where the patients learn skills to relate better to others so they can have more meaningful, intimate, rewarding relationships. They also learn about what emotions drive them to compete, distrust people, and how to cohabit a home, a workplace, or society in general in a healthier way.

These are people with NPD in a nutshell. It's a rare medical condition and people don't choose to have it. Today the word narcissism gets tossed around too carelessly. Many blogs and pseudoscientific articles talk about narcissistic behavior as if it would be full-blown NPD. They have a 99% chance to be wrong about their arbitrary, long-distance diagnosis. Yet, they can fire people up to label others as narcissists. Words have power. There's a difference when you tell someone "You're a narcissist." or "You behave in narcissistic ways."

That being said, people who don't have NPD (99% of the population) yet are at the far right end at the middle of the bell curve, can be extremely annoying and hard to deal with. They don't have a mental condition, they are just—in my opinion—people who don't know better, because for one reason or another they didn't learn better. From here onward, I would like to use the term self-absorbed to describe people who are exhibiting narcissistic traits yet are not clinically diagnosable with NPD.

The self-absorbed can be "cured," in theory, if they want to be cured—but often this is not the case. If you are dealing with someone like this in your life, be it a parent, a spouse, a friend, or loved one, know that it's not your job to save them. And also, you don't need to tolerate their often toxic, unhealthy ways of relating to you.

What Are the Self-Absorbed Made Of?

Whatever is true in the case of narcissists, a self-absorbed person can exhibit those traits, too, but in a milder, less frequent fashion, and while they might never admit it, they can feel remorse or regret.

The self-absorbed are those people who didn't learn to regulate their emotions well. They carry a lot of scars from their childhood but they don't know healthy coping mechanisms to deal with them. The more isolated these self-absorbed people are, the less likely they notice something's wrong with them. If everybody in their environment behaves the way they do, it's not surprising they will adopt the same unhealthy traits. They usually get the first big hit on their ego in school or at their workplace where there are many people. Some of these people will call them out on their self-centered, empathy-lacking, antisocial behavior. This is the point where the self-absorbed bump into a fork in the road—they may choose to believe the comments of their peers and try to change their unhealthy behavior and way of relating to others, or they may choose to respond to the "unfair attack" with defensiveness, counterattacking, gaslighting, or another defense mechanism.

The self-absorbed may feel unfairly attacked, as if the world was out to get them. From their perspective, their reaction actually makes sense. They learned one way to live in this world and to them that was the norm. Then someone comes along and tells them, "No, you are wrong, you should do it this way." One needs a great deal of self-control and self-reflection to not bite back to such a remark—and self-control and self-reflection are what the self-absorbed usually lack. I'm not trying to defend the behavior of the self-absorbed. I am, however, a recovering self-absorbed person, so

I can sympathize and understand where they are coming from as I came from the same place—and I needed 27 years to realize it.

Self-absorbed people don't necessarily have to be abused. Overly sheltered, overprotected, or spoiled kids can become self-absorbed just as much if not more than their less fortunate peers. Let me share with you my story of self-absorption and my way out of it.

I felt abandoned by my parents, which I often voiced by begging them not to leave me, so they strongly compensated for their lack of presence with presents. I was terribly, or perfectly, spoiled. My parents never discouraged me in anything, they never cut my wings. Unfortunately, they overcompensated here, too. I was too perfect, much better than anyone else in an exaggerated way. My parents were generous with me, giving the best bites of their food, the best of everything to me. They were showing me love this way but they failed to add an important message: "I give you my best bites because I'm your parent and I love you. But other people might not do this for you. And that doesn't mean they don't love you. They just show you love differently." So I started feeling entitled to the best of everything from others, and when they refused to give it to me I concluded they didn't love me. And, of course, I retaliated to the offense.

I was just a spoiled little brat with parents who they themselves never mastered the skills of self-reflection, self-improvement, emotional management, or a conscious, intentional way of living. Both of my parents are emotionally reactive. They can't manage their emotions in a healthy way; they explode. That was the pattern I grew up with, plus the princess syndrome.

Ever since I started school I felt the negative effect of these lacks in my upbringing. My classmates, teachers, my friends, and some of my boyfriends expressed their dislike of some aspects of my behavior which, as a well-trained self-absorbed person, I received with disbelief, defensiveness, and contempt. Was I a bad, malicious person? No. But I acted in unloving, unkind ways, which hurt the people around me. Maybe due to the law of attraction, I failed at witnessing healthy behavior patterns from emotionally mature people. Maybe because they were emotionally mature, and they didn't bother with diamonds in the rough like myself. I only attracted people who were just like me in some other messed up way.

And then I read the book *Adult Children of Emotionally Immature Parents*, gaining access to a plethora of information that was previously unknown to me, and then I started digging and learning. And digging some more, and learning some more. My core is pure and wants to be a good, loving, caring, kind person. I finally found the path to it: books. The memories, knowledge, and experiences of healthy people I want to resemble. It's not my fault my parents didn't teach me better values. It's not their fault either; they did the best they could. But ever since I tapped into the well of knowledge and I became aware of the serious gaps in my character development, it became my responsibility to fill these gaps.

I was 27 when I started. My best friend (call it the law of similar attracts similar) was 37 when he tapped into his well of awareness and started changing for the better. My point is, it's never too late. You can rewire your brain, fill in the gaps your parenting left in you, and live in a more emotionally mature way.

However you thought, reacted, or acted in the past, you can change it. If you desire to be called out on your stuff, if you wish to stop and take a hard look at your reactions and take ownership of them, it means that you're not doomed to be a self-absorbed person or a narcissist. You're actually quite the opposite. You just need guidance.

First you need to find a role model you wish to learn from. This role model can be anyone. To me it was about 15 great books—whoever was described in them. If you wish, I can share my list of books with you, just send me an email. What worked for me might not be the best fit for you. I found these books by inserting my problems in Google's search engine and by searching Amazon's book selection with the keywords "narcissism," "emotional immaturity," "overreacting," "lack of emotional control," and so on. Also, I found real gems in the list of references of some of the books I really loved. Having no person to model isn't a valid excuse today. Books are accessible, you can read, and you can take action out of free will. And then the law of attraction will work its magic for you. The more emotionally mature, empathetic, and loving you become, the more of these people you will start to attract. I'm speaking from genuine experience.

Toxic people and relationships tend to bring out the worst in us. If you feel that you are a generally caring person, who is compassionate and a great listener, yet with your partner or parents you feel quite the opposite—or these people experience you in a totally different way—it means that there is discord. You need space from such influence. Some days when I talk to LE he still can bring the worst out of me even though I know and I do better now. Our messy relationships have one use: to show us those many things we still need to improve on.

But the work we're doing on ourselves is what's really adding to our personal growth. If you reach a point where you love the person you are, with yourself and others, embrace it. This means locking out those people who bring out the worst in you and make you feel unloving with yourself and others.

Chapter 6: Gaslighting

I would like to introduce you to a common manipulation method closely related to the self-absorbed or narcissists. It's called gaslighting. Did you see the movie *Gaslight*? It's a classic movie from the 1940s where a husband tries to convince his wife that she's insane by making her question her reality. This is what gaslighting is all about, it is "a form of persistent manipulation and brainwashing that causes the victim to doubt her or himself, and to ultimately lose one's own sense of perception, identity, and self-worth."[xii]

Gaslighters come in many shapes and forms. Those who purposefully, with bad intentions, lure their victims into a belief only to question it later and play with the victim's sense of sanity, usually have some kind of personality disorder like narcissism. We can, however, gaslight our loved ones without meaning it or noticing it. Yet the act can be damaging to the relationship in the long run.

How do you detect gaslighting? In the beginning, you may start to feel confused and doubt yourself around the gaslighter. They will try to convince you that your memories, emotions, and thoughts are invalid or wrong. If you don't agree with them, the gaslighter may become angry, passive aggressive, or outright mean, and will try to twist the truth to their advantage. They might try to make you to be the bad guy, and make you believe that they are actually victimized by you. As time goes by, you, the real victim, will find it more and more difficult to trust your own senses and separate the truth from the gaslighter's manipulative story.

In the last one and a half year of our relationship, LE and I gaslit each other regularly—I'm fairly sure, unwittingly. Yet, these little episodes just further damaged our already fragile bond.

For example, we had a conversation one day about what was wrong in our relationship. LE said that the problem was that I was taking things very personally and he felt he was walking on eggshells around me and couldn't be himself. I replied that I could see why he felt that way, yet it was hard to not take things personally when I'm literally pointed fingers at while receiving harsh criticism with a cold tone.

The next day when this topic came up again we hit a wall. LE told me matter-of-factly that the day before, I agreed with him that the problem was me taking things personally; why was I denying this fact when yesterday I already acknowledged that he was right? I was absolutely convinced that I said something along the lines of, "I can see why, from your perspective, your opinion makes sense…" LE chose to interpret this statement as me agreeing with him. And he became so upset and insistent that I started questioning my memory and sanity. Did I really say or not say that?

LE came at me with an overt casting of blame that made me defensive—and I acted in a self-protective way. My reaction only assured him that he was right and that I do take everything personally. I wasn't loving either as I failed to validate his pain. I started with the courtesy sentence of "I can see why this makes sense to you…" but then I threw the ball back in his court with covert blaming. While I told him the exact reason why I was defensive, he couldn't internalize it. He was entangled too deeply in his own story and pain—he just wanted his misery to stop and his best way to defend himself against the pain, he felt, was to tell me harshly to stop doing what hurt him: defensiveness. I was entangled in my own pain story—"If you stop blaming me, I won't get defensive."—I defended myself by telling him what I needed. Both of us were right and none of us were. Can you see how messy relationship dynamics can get? There was no bad guy or good guy there, we were two sides of the same coin.

The air was filled with tension, we expressed and repressed pain and contempt against each other. This mental state is a fertile ground for gaslighting. So the next time the painful topic came up LE blurted out that I said something I didn't say. I'm sure he didn't mean to make me feel crazy but sometimes, when angry and emotionally overcharged, we can make the mistake of gaslighting. This is why it's always better to have difficult conversations when we are calm and collected. Under tension our judgment gets clouded and we put our wall of defense mechanisms high up. Using gaslighting as a defense, "You didn't say that." or "I didn't say that." can happen easily.

Here's a tip on how to avoid gaslighting. First, make sure that both of you are generally well-meaning, good-hearted people, who don't have the intention of hurting each other. If you suspect you gaslighter is doing it on purpose, absolutely disengage from the conversation and even from the relationship. If, however, you are just the typical case of good people doing bad things, you could consider doing the following:

Operate from a premise of love and curiosity, but don't let yourself get lost in the crazy-making cycle if you're absolutely certain you did or didn't say something. Let's see in my case with LE how we could have done better:

LE: Yesterday you said that you agree with me!
Me: I'm sorry but I remember it differently. Can you recall what I said?
LE: Well, I don't remember, but I know you agreed!
Me: Can I tell you how I remember it?
LE: Sure.
Me: I remember saying that I can see why you feel the way you feel. By this I meant that I find your emotions valid and your reaction understandable. But this doesn't mean I agree with my behavior being the only or main problem in our relationship.
LE: I never said it was.

Me: Okay, then I guess we misunderstood each other. Is it clearer now what I meant yesterday?
LE: Yes.

Let's break down what happened here.

1. When someone comes at you with a strong belief in their truth, the worst you can do is tell them they are wrong. That sentence makes people instantly defensive.
2. Instead of questioning LE's truth, I only stated my truth: that I remember things differently.
3. Throw the ball back to the other person's court using curiosity and a tone of kind or neutral inquiry. Make sure to ask why the other party thinks what they think. Asking about LE's recollection of the facts is a good way

to see where the communication went south.

4. Be prepared to receive a fact-avoiding answer. "I just know." or "I don't remember the exact words but…"

5. This is a good place to be because the person who unwittingly gaslit you due to over-fueled emotions will—hopefully—hear their gaps in the story. When they have this crack on their conviction shield, just kindly ask to share your part in the story. A well-meaning person whose primary objective is to solve the problem will want to hear you out. If they don't want to hear you out, well, that's also telltale information—it means they only care about protecting their side. If this is the case, there's not much you can achieve with logic or kindness. The best action to take here is walking away from the

situation in a loving way. "I feel we can't get to a common ground right now. I really want to talk about this and solve this problem with you when we're both in the right headspace. Let's just resume this talk another time."

6. Let's assume the other party is open to hear you out. Now is your chance to explain what you really meant and felt. Stay clear of "you" sentences, use "I" sentences instead. Be honest about how you feel but be gentle in your delivery. If the other person, again, is genuinely interested in fixing the problem, they will accept your reasoning. You know better what you meant, after all. If LE was gaslighting me willfully, he would have stuck to his guns and express his disbelief even when I told him what I really meant. He was sulking but he let

go of the belief that he knew better than me about what I meant.
7. Make sure to get verbal confirmation about you two being on the same page about the issue. Just ask your conversation partner if they understand you better now or if they require further explanation. Based on their reply you can continue the talk in a similarly calm and collected fashion.

This process can be easier said than done when you're facing hostility from the other party. Gaslighting is usually just the symptom of a deeper underlying problem in a relationship or in one's character. As I said before, in severe and willful cases, gaslighting can be a sign that you're dealing with someone who has NPD or another personality disorder. In mild, involuntary cases gaslighting reveals that something is broken in your relationship. LE and I had lots of things broken between us which we couldn't fix. We didn't gaslight because we wanted to hurt each other, we were just hurting and didn't know better.

I started reading about gaslighting around the time when our relationship was beyond repair. Today I know better. Just like with anything else in this book, awareness, knowledge, and a strong desire to improve are needed first and foremost—and then everything can be changed.

Did you just discover that you've gaslit your loved ones before? I'm stating this with full certainty, we all have. What matters is that you know better now. Apologize to your loved ones and commit to not gaslight again. Plus, if you suspect some underlying problems in your relationship, also commit to talk about it with your partner (or parents, or friends). If you find communication rusty between the two of you, try to suggest couples or family therapy and work on your issues there.

No toxic habit is unchangeable as long as both parties are genuinely interested in overcoming them. Similarly, no toxic dynamic is changeable as long as only one party is aware of the problems and works on themself. It takes two to tango.

Chapter 7: Abandonment Issues

Have you ever felt needy of love, affection, or the physical presence of someone? Are you ever labeled clingy? Do you fear being abandoned by your partner more than is "normal"? Are you often anxious about keeping people in your life?

If you answered yes to any of these questions, you may have abandonment issues. Some people develop this problem for obvious reasons: the death of a parent, being chronically neglected, having a parent who has bipolar disorder and therefore changeable mood and expectations, and so on. But some people develop abandonment issues for nonobvious reasons like poverty; even if the parents were present in the child's life, consistent lacking in meeting basic physical needs may translate into the fear that emotional resources are also limited.

Abandonment issues manifest in two ways, either in needy, anxious, clingy behavior patterns, or in distant, avoidant, and shallow connection patterns. Both of these types of people have the same goal in mind: protect themselves from the pain of abandonment; just one copes by becoming overly clingy, the other copes by not forming meaningful relationships at all. They follow the "If I don't have it, I have nothing to lose." logic.

John Bowlby, a British psychologist, pioneered in his research about child development and their attachment styles, developing a new focus of psychology called attachment theory. Attachment theory attempts to describe the dynamics of long-term and short-term interpersonal relationships between humans, addressing only a specific area, namely "how humans respond in relationships when hurt, separated from loved ones, or perceiving a threat."[xiii] Bowlby discovered that the need for young children to develop attachments to their primary caretakers was the effect of evolutionary pressures, because attachment behavior would help the infant's survival in the face of dangers.[xiv]

The most important observation of attachment theory is that the child needs to develop a secure, healthy bond with at least one parent for their own successful social and emotional development and emotional regulation. If this secure attachment bond isn't formed, the child will diverge from the ideal secure attachment style and will present one of the insecure attachment styles. A person can carry their attachment style into adulthood. But our early-gained attachment style isn't a life sentence—we can change it with awareness and work. This statement, however, can work both ways. One who grew up in a healthy family and formed a secure attachment style can develop an insecure attachment style later in life due to unhealthy relationships or great traumas. Let's take a look at the different adult attachment styles developed by John Bowlby and Mary Ainsworth:

1. **Secure**

People with a secure attachment style have a positive view of themself and of others. They form close connections relatively easily without any fearful thoughts about them. They are comfortable depending on others and others depending on them. They view themselves as genuinely adequate, don't worry about not being enough or that they will never be loved again if they lose a partner. They are okay both with intimacy and independence. Securely attached people are warm and responsive to emotional needs and are good at regulating both positive and negative emotions.

2. Anxious-preoccupied

People who have an anxious-preoccupied attachment style have a negative self-image and a positive image of others. They want to get close to others but often experience that others may not want to get as close in return. They want to have close relationships but often ruminate about others not caring as much about them as they care about others. They have a high need for validation, approval, and responsiveness from their surroundings. They can become overly dependent on their partners, parents, or friends. Anxiously attached people may have a poor opinion about themselves which is eased only when they are around their attachment figure. In terms of emotional regulation, they are reactive, impulsive, and emotionally overly expressive.

3. Dismissive-avoidant

This type of attachment style comes with a high opinion of self and a low opinion of others. Dismissive-avoidants claim they are happy without having close emotional relationships, finding them unimportant. Independence and self-sufficiency is something they highly value. Dependence of any form makes them feel uncomfortable. Their desire for independence, however, may be a way to avoid attachment. They tend to hide or suppress their feelings and use distancing as a coping mechanism for rejection.[xv]

4. Fearful-avoidant

People with fearful-avoidant attachment style have an unstable, changeable, confused view of self and others. Those who suffered sever trauma in their life (like sexual abuse) are more prone to belong to this attachment style. They long for close emotional relationships but they are afraid of them at the same time. They worry they might get hurt. They distrust the attachments of others, and can see themselves as unworthy of a close bond anyway. They are in a constant mixed-feeling zone but they lean towards suppressing their emotions rather than being expressive about them. They also struggle showing genuine intimacy and caring even though they feel positively about someone.[xvi]

As I mentioned before, you don't need to settle for any attachment style if you don't like it. A secure attachment style only needs maintenance—congratulations, you won the lottery ticket of life. The other three styles need us to dig a bit deeper in our psyche and consciously do things to change them. In this chapter I will focus on abandonment issues as the reason for any insecure attachment style.

To start working on your abandonment issues you need to bring them out of the shadows and into the conversational light. And you continue by getting as closely familiar with your process as you can. You know, getting to know yourself, what you're doing, and how you're doing in this emotional department.

For example, you want to get clear on what you do to maintain your relationships' security. What are the "manipulations" you have learned to do? What have your strategies been? Be honest and make sure you are uncovering all of these things. In a twelve-step program, people refer to this part as "taking a fearless moral inventory." Bring all the abandonment prevention methods into your conscious awareness, and become able to identify and describe them to yourself.

For example, when my partner says something negative to me, I tend to use an ultimatum to show them that I hold more power in the relationship. When my partner told me about my bad habit of interrupting them and listening poorly, I left the room and started collecting my clothes saying, "If you don't like me that much, I can leave." This is an extreme example. I only offer it so you have a clear idea what abandonment prevention methods can entail. Sometimes they are quite counterintuitive, as this example. "I don't want to get abandoned, so I threaten to abandon you so you get scared and don't leave me." This, by the way, is a very toxic coping mechanism, and if you tend to do something similar, I'd suggest getting it on your radar pronto. Why do you do this? What goal do you wish to achieve with this behavior? What emotions trigger this behavior? Where did you see this coping method and how did you feel about it at your earliest exposure? And so on. You can ask these same questions about milder abandonment prevention tactics, too.

Working on abandonment issues needs you to examine the worst-case scenario of your fears. Instead of sinking in the fear of being abandoned, put your focus on all the things that could or would happen if or when you get abandoned. Make an inventory of your thoughts. Some of these thoughts and emotions might be more like an app running in the background—not necessarily part of your conscious thinking. You need to really dig deep and come up with every possible concern or perspective that you live with about being abandoned by your relationship partner or any other person you care about. Some of these fears are kept alive more by your inner child than your adult self. But at the end of the day it doesn't matter where they're coming from, if they're part of your psyche, they matter and need your attention.

A third thing you can do when you're wrestling with abandonment issues is to use your imagination to try and see if you can create an ideal person who doesn't have abandonment issues. What would this person think about their relationship partner leaving them? What would they think of the idea of being abandoned? What might their perspective and thoughts be? How might they look at the whole idea of their relationship coming to an end?

This practice takes some effort and creativity because you're positioning yourself into the shoes of someone who thinks and feels differently than you do. What might that be like? What might their perspective be when they don't harbor any big fears about being left? Can you imagine…?

There is another way of being than feeling constantly terrified by being abandoned. This other way may seem out of reach for you at the moment, but it's possible. It is the way of "letting go." By letting go, I don't mean "letting go" of the person per se, but rather letting go of being attached to the outcome, the panic, and your desire to want to control the outcome of your situation. You might say, "But I am fighting for what I believe in, I believe in us!" That passion and dedication is good; but here I'm talking about letting go of the will-they-stay-or-will-they-leave misery that cripples your mind. Letting go is a form of release. A sense of trust in yourself that you will be okay, no matter how much your heart hurts.

I won't lie, breakups happen sometimes. But you can choose to look at them differently. You may decide to lovingly separate for the moment from someone with the intention to heal; to find yourselves (again) and learn to navigate life as individuals. You can keep each other in your hearts, and if you feel that you changed enough and you divert towards each other, reconnect, and try again, now better at being more authentic and grounded as individuals… Ideally, this is the healthy state that people ought to arrive at when they become aware of one or both partners having resistance to being in the relationship.

But with attachment, fear of abandonment, the fear of making a mistake, and societal expectations, couples tend to stay together when it no longer feels good, or safe. Not to say that relationships should feel amazing all the time, because that's not realistic, but being in the relationship should feel like a place where both of you want to be. And if that feeling changes, it's time to implement a separation.

Pleasing Others out of Fear of Abandonment

People pleasing sometimes gets such a bad reputation. The fact that we want to "be good for someone" has some underlying emotions and belief systems triggering it, but wanting to please one's partner or loved one is not a bad wish in general. It's especially healthy when both people in the relationship—romantic or another kind—share this wish to please the other.

"I love you." really means "I love how I feel when I'm with you." It's interesting that the concept of loving how you feel when you are with a person is actually seeing yourself through your partner's eyes. If that view is a good one, then the reflection back to oneself is good. And if that view is discouraging in some way, it's a natural tendency to start to internalize that reflection of oneself, to the point of believing that one is "less than." That is the power of relationships: when you open your heart and make yourself vulnerable emotionally.

Chapter 8: The Mind-Changing Magic of Meditation

LE had a list of reasons why I was not a good match for him. He called them potential deal breakers. He even made a drawing in my journal explaining the level of my acceptability in his assessment. His key deal breakers were these, among others:

> - "You are not a native English speaker, which naturally puts a cap on our communication ability and friendship."

While I could understand why this could be a problem to someone, I didn't understand the timeline of the idea. I was just as much of a native speaker four years ago as I was that day.

If anything, my English had only improved. The cruelty of this deal breaker laid in its fatalistic nature. I will never be an American-born English speaker. There's simply nothing I can do about it.

- "You don't know yourself."

What the heck does that even mean? Know thyself. In a philosophical way? In a Buddhist way? Who am I? The being who is thinking or the one who notices that she's thinking? Who's noticing, then? Right? It's such a broad and confusing statement. I know I like sushi…

I was confused. After extensive talks about this topic, I understood what he meant: I don't really have a solid idea on what I want to do in life, what I prefer for myself. I was mostly doing what he wanted. He was right about me not having any authority over my needs as I was very much terrified of disobeying him.

In the months that I only now consider unconscious uncoupling, I was very anxious about "finding myself." To please him, of course. To remove this barrier out of the way of our happily ever after. So I did journaling, and I read, and I thought, and I journaled some more. But I couldn't really nail down who I was that fit his description of knowledge of identity. My mistake was that even though I thought I was thinking independently, I operated from a premise that I knew he approved; I couldn't be anything I knew he would disapprove of. So all that self-assessment was in vain. I desperately tried to fit a puzzle I was not cut for instead of putting together my own puzzle.

Weirdly enough, LE told me that as long as we were together, I wouldn't be able to "find who I am." He was right about this. When we are emotionally enmeshed with another person, it's really hard—if not impossible—to think for ourselves. This is why having a break in a relationship—not just a romantic one, but any relationship that has significant influence over us—can be beneficial. This is what that vague "need for space" means. It's not so much about the physical space but the mental space, the emotional space. Where you can discover that all your worst-case scenarios about abandonment, inadequacy, and loneliness were so untrue. Where you can be with yourself and finally build up that solid life plan you always wanted.

If you are affected by an emotionally abusive partner, parent, or friend, you could consider taking the space needed for you to think clearly.

I had a cool conversation with my mom on how we can answer the "Who am I?" question, and what we concluded was this: "I am the compilation of my experiments, experiences, memories, and knowledge of today. Every day." I love this answer to one of humanity's biggest existential dilemma. Even if you know how your mind works, how and why your emotions pop up, how you manage things under pressure, what your favorite meal at Burger King is… the knowledge of these things only amounts to as much as you can use of it moment by moment. And no two moments are the same. One moment you act according to the "self-knowledge" blueprint. The next moment you act out of character. It happens. We even say, "You're not yourself." But then who are you? Did you just cease to exist for those moments you were not yourself? Of course not. That's you, too. When you're not yourself.

When you're yourself (by self-definition). All the time, moment by moment.

I think it's much more constructive to think in terms of self-concept. I know, it's hard to have one when you grew up with parents who struggled with their own self-concepts.

How Do You Develop a Solid Self-Concept in Adulthood?

As we grow, mature, and try to develop our best selves, our need grows. We start forming a solid sense of self as infants. Ideally, our mother or primary caretaker reflects back what we are doing: smiling, wondering, meeting our cries with empathy. Thus we get to feel validated, important. This validation helps us as babies to draw some conclusions unconsciously, like "I matter, I am worthy of attention, to be cared for—I'm enough the way

I am." When we don't receive this reflection, for whatever reason, we won't feel validated, and as a consequence, we don't develop a solid sense of self. We instead learn to focus on others and ignore ourselves.

This process, unfortunately, is a common event in the world and it explains why it is so common to have an underdeveloped sense of self. Fear not, this is not an unchangeable fact. You can add new chapters to your origin story (which involves the unsolidified sense of self) with awareness and understanding that this is just how your life got started, but it doesn't have to define your life—you can start finding your real self. The authentic you, who you are moment by moment, is worthy, lovable, and matters. And there are many people who'll be delighted to get to know you. The real you.

Mindfulness can be a helpful ally in your self-concept solidification. I regularly practice mindfulness meditation in my days for almost two years now. In the beginning I was honestly convinced that it wouldn't help me to sit in silence, trying to accept and let go of my thoughts. For weeks I was practicing, and since I was very dedicated, I made some improvements in not scratching my backside when it was itching; just calmly noticing the sensation, not judging the event, just say *itching* and then breathe in and breathe out the experience without being reactive. I also observed what obsessive thoughts popped up in my mind when I sat in silence—which were the ones that left easily, and which were the ones that needed more embracing.

Without noticing, I became better at releasing negative thoughts, even the ones that seemed the scariest at the time. Just kept returning to my breath over and over again without judgment. I noticed, for example, that I don't use negative, shaming self-talk on myself by default. This realization soothed me a bit. Slowly I got more familiar with how my brain works, and since I was in a silent, undisturbed place I could practice some metacognition—thinking about my thoughts. Meditation opened my thinking brain to my observing brain. It was a slow process, I didn't wake up the second day feeling, "I know myself." My intention wasn't even to get to know myself when I started meditating, rather I wanted to become less reactive.

Decreased reactivity is another great byproduct of meditation, by the way. The first time I felt how beneficial my regular daily practice was on a Saturday afternoon, about seven months into meditating. LE said something that normally would have triggered a knee-jerk reaction of me, but not this time. There was a brief moment where somewhere in the back of my brain I translated the emotion into words: "irritation." And immediately I fired out a command: "breathe." And so I did. You know those scenes in a movie where the main character experiences some kind of cathartic discovery, and the camera starts zooming in on them while the outside noises and sights become blurry and tuned down? That's exactly how I felt. LE kept talking but I stopped paying attention to him. This experience to me was a huge step. It was the catalyst of my shifting beliefs about myself. I used to tell myself, "I'm emotionally reactive, that's who I am. I can't do anything about that." And in that moment I first learned about myself... "Yes, I can."

To me meditation was and is a life-altering skill. It empowered me, helped me shed some unhelpful beliefs about myself, and opened up the gates to mental peace. I honestly hope it can do that for you, too. Let me walk you through exactly what I did to turn my sinking mental ship around.

1. Meditation Boot Camp

Day one, I decided that I wanted to try this meditation thing. I went fishing with my dad that day at a beautiful lake. Fishing was our bonding activity ever since I was a kid; my enthusiasm about it, however, decreased year by year. My dad can be very excited about holding his fishing rod and I sat quietly on a bench. That's when the aha moment came to me: I want to meditate.

I won't lie, I did it with help. I downloaded an app called *Calm* to my phone and they offered a one-month trial. "Why not? What do I have to lose?" I thought. I started their 7 Days of Calm introductory meditation course. This is exactly what it sounds: for seven days you get a new guided meditation audio to complete. Then you can advance to their 21 Days of Calm course. While they have situation-specific guided meditations—for sleep, for anxiety, stress release, and so on—I'd highly recommend you start with these two courses as they help you enormously with easy techniques and at the end of the twenty-eight days, if you don't feel like purchasing a membership, you'll still be good to go and try meditating on your own.

I went on with *Calm* loving every moment of my meditation practice. I did the course episode in the morning and one of their sleeping aid body scan meditations in the evening. So I meditated about twenty minutes per day. Every day.

2. Meditation Level Two

Seven months later, when I was living in Taiwan, I joined a meditation group. By that time I had seven months' worth of meditation under my belt and I had my big breakthroughs I told you about. Being a curious creature, I wanted to level up my meditation game as I could clearly see its benefits. I'm not a spiritual person by default but belonging to this group made me feel more grounded and connected to myself and to the world than ever before. I felt safe there. It was the first time in my life I felt like I belonged. I understood finally what all the hullabaloo was about belonging to a community where you may be the most diverse people in the world yet you are all bonded by a shared value. (And no, it was not a cult, before you ask.)

Trying to meditate on my own (without my guided meditation app crutch) was easier than I thought. Sitting together with thirty other people who are all very focused and disciplined certainly helps. There is a strange peaceful energy floating around and one can feel our shared humanity.

I can't recommend enough to you to find a meditation group in your community and start practicing together. Beyond the obvious benefits of the meditation itself, you'll meet amazingly cool people. I might have a narrow experience but I will still share it: the great thing about meditation groups is that no one goes to one who is not even a little bit in touch with themself. Or if they aren't, they have a strong desire to be. In other words, they are on the same path as you. Sharing our journey of self-discovery with each other is in itself healing and helpful. I often had to cry when I heard basically my story from someone else's mouth. "You too? I'm not the only one?" You look at each other, hug each other, and cry. No words are needed as you both know what the other must feel and go through. There is a tremendous healing power in finding a soul sister or brother—even if you only meet for a day.

3. Meditation Mogul

Almost one year after my first meditation experience and exactly four days after breaking up with LE, I started the "pray" part of my tiny eat-pray-love journey. I went to a meditation camp in France. Let me repeat, I'm not really a spiritual person, and while I don't reject the existence of God, I'm not an avid practitioner of faith. But… but this must have been God's work. I booked my meditation camp in February or March in 2019. The camp itself started on the 11th of July. I had no idea that by the time I went to the camp I'd be single for four days. Yet it was the best timing for this experience.

The meditation camp is called Plum Village and it was founded by Thich Nath Hahn. Yes, that Thich Nath Hahn. The only one. It started as a refugee camp for people who escaped the horrors of the Vietnam War, but as things calmed down, this beautiful spot on the French Riviera became the main hub of Thich Nath Hahn's mindfulness teachings. Today it is one of the most highly rated meditation retreats—and I can certainly reinforce that.

Needless to say, I was at rock bottom. Being freshly ditched (yes, I got dumped) after working hard for almost a year to save my relationship… What am I doing here? What I felt so deeply in my meditation group in

Taiwan, the sense of belonging and togetherness, well, I didn't feel it here. Cheerful nuns with big smiles on their faces were walking around, helping the flow of people find their homes on the small campus. Children ran around cheerfully, becoming friends with each other. People were chatting, smiling. I didn't get it. Ain't anybody suffering? I sure as hell was. I wanted my bed. I wanted to leave.

When a tiny black-haired woman came to my aid, I felt relief. I could finally hide inside my bed and cry. Her "aid" was not that great. After checking out almost every wooden house, we finally found mine. I cynically thought to myself, "I feel like I gave the tour to this lady who works here by checking out every hut on campus." My roommates were sleeping in their beds. At two p.m. Great. Now I needed to cry in silence.

I wasn't so lucky, as once I put down my stuff the little black-haired woman urged me to go back to the main campus and choose a family. Family? What is this, Gandhi's Godfather gig? I scraped my name under the family *Lotus Pond* as they had only a few people. "The smaller the family the better," I thought. "Can I get lost now?" Little did I know that each family had an assigned task for the entire duration of their stay. And Lotus Pond happened to be the dishwasher family. People seemed to know this—that's why not many signed up there. *This can't be worse... This can't be worse...* Actually, it could be. It turned out we had to be on duty before and after every meal, a total of six times a day, and wash all the dishes. There were 400 people on campus, not counting the nuns and the volunteers. Did you see the Disney movie *Hercules*? There is a scene when Hades discovers that his faithful minions are wearing *Hercules'* merchandise and he explodes in anger. That's exactly how I felt.

The first day was terrible. I was in no mood to wash dishes, to chat with people, or to socialize. All I wanted was to meditate away that bloody heartache I was feeling. *That's why I came here! I want to be alone, I want to meditate, or hum, or chant, or whatever you people do and heal! So better do your magic, soul witches!*

There's a saying that sometimes in life what you need is not what you want. Yet it's okay to meet the unwanted with initial resistance. It doesn't make you a bad person, just human.

I learned that day firsthand that it's okay to allow yourself to be skeptical and cynical for a while as long as you keep your heart open.

The second day we woke up at 5:30 to go to morning meditation at six a.m. Feeling the first rays of the sun warming my skin in the serene meditation hall I shared with 400 other people was the first moment something moved in me. When I went to my kitchen duty I looked at my fellow dishwashers with different eyes. They were tired too. Some had puffy eyes; they probably cried themselves to sleep. Yet they washed the dishes without any complaint. "Be in the here and now. Be grateful for your hands that can wash these dishes. Be happy for the food that lays in your stomach," said our head sister, I guess the Godmother. I gave up my cynicism. *Since I'm here, I might as well just do what they say. Maybe they know better.* And for sure they did.

This day I learned firsthand the tremendous soul-freeing power of surrender. Life becomes easier even in the most unwanted circumstances if you start flowing with the current.

The third day I woke up ten minutes before anyone else. I went to the kitchen to fill the washing buckets with water so we didn't have to deal with that when the dishes started piling up. I jumped in the line of the cleaning process wherever I was needed. (Before, I only liked putting the dishes into the sanitizing machine.) My family was very grateful for the head start and we could finish our tasks about 15 minutes quicker. Our Godmother proposed to spend the remaining time having an ice cream and playing some games. It was a lovely sunny day, and we'd enjoy the ice cream so much after the sweaty chores of washing about 1000 plates and who knows how many utensils.

I learned that day firsthand that giving is more rewarding for the soul than receiving.

From day four I started being mindful of the work of the other groups, the cooks, the organizers, the compost group, the restroom group. I tried my best to live my life in a way to cause as little trouble and work for them as possible. I even started doing tasks that were not mine because... why not?

In the afternoons we had an activity called Dharma Talk. I thought that this was some kind of reading gig, but no. Our family would sit in a circle and everyone who wanted to share something about themselves, could. I felt anxious. *What should I share? What should I share? Something cool? Something sad? Something tragic? I have all these topics up my sleeve.* There is always tension when you need to speak about yourself in front of strangers. A girl two seats ahead of me silently spoke up as if she read my thoughts.

"I feel a great pressure now," she said, "to say something interesting to you guys. The thing is, I don't think I'm interesting. And being around people makes me fearful day and night. What do they think of me? Will they judge me? Do they think I'm stupid? Do you think I'm stupid? I feel so insecure. I just constantly feel I'm not enough."

What a courageous person! Her name is Amanda, she is 22 years old and she showed more self-knowledge, courage, and authenticity than many beyond her age. Many of us broke into tears—myself included. She spoke for all of us. Being afraid, she stood up and she spoke her truth. You bet no one thought she was stupid or not enough. We looked at her in amazement, respect, and admiration. Amanda was our hero. Amanda, if you read this, you're amazing and I wrote a book about you! Please keep sharing your amazing self with the world.

I learned that day firsthand that vulnerability is not weakness, it's strength.

On day five I cheerfully woke up before my alarm went off. I ran to the kitchen to prepare the dishwashing water only to see that two of my other family members were also there preparing it already. It warmed my heart. We went to our morning meditation and I continued my day high-spirited.

That day I learned firsthand the blessing of reciprocity. What you give is what you get. When you give good, you receive good.

On day six we decided we wanted to perform a song as a family at the upcoming moon festival, which was organized on the last day of the camp. We'd do our chores, we'd do our mediation, our Dharma talk, and in our resting time, we'd put our heads and talents together and rewrite the song "Moon River" into a meditation medley. We had guitar players, drummers, a flute, good singers, and enthusiastic singers. Granddads, youngsters, people with special needs, nuns, and the rest of the bunch worked together as one to create something together. The song we wrote was wonderful and we enjoyed each moment of the process of creation.

That day I learned firsthand that the best memories in life really don't cost a thing.

On our last day we all felt a bit blue. We grew fond of each other and our life at the camp. By this point we perfected our dishwashing technique so we'd finish work early each time and we'd hang out sharing our life with one another, being validated and listened to. Some of us—myself included—would "test" on a mindfulness training, called Five Mindfulness Training, and get certified. We'd all get a Dharma name chosen by our Godmother based on her assessment about our behavior in the past few days. My Dharma name is "Compassionate Action of the Heart." I cried when I received it.

When I arrived to the camp on day one, I was everything but compassionate. I was way too absorbed in my own pain. And yet slowly through all those hours of meditation, of dishwashing, of talking with the amazing people I met, my pain transformed into something greater. There is something in the idea that when you feel you need help, help someone else and your soul will heal. I didn't feel like the most misfortunate creature there. I didn't even feel misfortunate, rather blessed. I haven't shed a tear for LE ever since that camp. I made total peace with our breakup. I understood we weren't meant to be. And I also experienced that there is so much more out there to focus on than a failed relationship. So many things can spark joy in one's heart. There is so much more to who we are than our reflection in someone else's eye. I learned to love my beautiful self for who I was each moment and accepted that LE simply couldn't do it. I felt loved, I was loved. I was love. I am love. And so are you.

Plum Village offers the best meditation camp out there for sure. I didn't understand why on my first day but it was crystal clear on my last… Don't believe me? Go and experience it for yourself.

That week I learned firsthand that healing is not a solitary, self-focused act. Healing and happiness comes when it's shared.

Chapter 9: On Shaming, Blaming, and Criticizing

If you had parents or partners who were really good at observing and assessing critically, and then sharing with you their observations, it may take some time to work through the scars these remarks left on you and put them into an objective perspective. Was their sharing accurate? Maybe... But harmful to loving, close relationships and your self-esteem? For sure.

A crucial aspect about receiving criticism from another person is whether or not we actually believe that what they're telling us is true. If we do not believe, or at least partially believe, their remarks to be true, we might be inclined to dismiss what they said as nonsense, or tune them out, or respond by telling them that their attempts to critique us are disturbing. But if instead their words find their way down to the innermost part of our soul, we'll feel emotional pain.

Especially if we don't have a good grasp on who and how we are, we may tell ourselves "If they're seeing it and saying it, it must be true." or "I'm not loveable because of these things that they're pointing out to me." or "I'm inadequate so I better try harder to please them…" and so on.

Now, I challenge you to challenge these beliefs. Are they really true? Just because that one person said it? Think about why their criticism touched you so much. What soft spot did they touch? Become clear on the things that make you feel guilty or ashamed or inadequate and know what those things are. From there, it's easier to dig deeper about each of those things and really inspect whether they are truly "true" or not.

Michelle, my therapist, once told me that self-assessment—as opposed to having someone else doing the assessing; criticizing, in other words—comes down to an analysis of determining whether or not these qualities that make you feel guilty or inadequate are fine as they are or if they need to be changed or eliminated.

You can ask yourself, "Is this thing a part of who I am that I need to accept, and others need to accept too if they want to be with me? Or is this thing something that is perhaps unhealthy or limiting, or not in alignment with the person I want to be?"

If the answer is yes to the latter, then it's a matter of giving it enough attention to adopt new, healthier ways of being. You can do it. Guilt is our inbuilt alarm system. It tells us that something is not in alignment with who we are or who we want to be. So if guilt is invading, we can use that as guidance for getting some clarification on whether new lessons and practices need to be learned, or rather, whether new self-acceptance needs to be attained.

When we are criticized our natural, organic "issues" that we carry around with us from childhood may be labeled as bad, wrong, or dysfunctional. Let's take the label "needy" as an example. Such observations can lead us to think that there is something wrong with wanting to be accepted or seeking approval from others. Wanting the acceptance of a partner or a parent is not a dysfunction, nor is wanting their approval. But in some relationships, wanting or needing approval and acceptance is problematic because of all the layers of emotional dynamics and triggers that may drive the two of you. But just a general overall desire to be cherished, valued, accepted, and so on by your loved ones is not a bad thing.

Can you see how damaging criticism can get? Your traits that are "problematic" for one person are not necessarily problematic in life, or in general.

When someone is shaming you and blaming you simultaneously, they repeatedly hold you accountable for something you did wrong in their view. But instead of talking this issue out once and agreeing on a method of resolution, they just keep bringing up the old offenses as a broken record. They might use it as an ace in their deck every time they want to have the final word in an argument. Cheating is a classic example of the shame-blame card. By no means do I approve of cheating, but if the cheated party accepts to try to restore the relationship, using the cheat card every time to trump the person who cheated creates a toxic loop and will devastate both people. In such cases the best thing is to release the relationship—temporarily or for good.

When people blame so harshly, what they try to do is get away from their own shame and inflict it onto another. People who suffer from alcoholism, let's say, might do this more often. For example, the person with alcohol problems drank again, and their partner calls the bad behavior out, saying, "Your drinking really makes me feel uncomfortable. I so wish we could do something about it." The person with addiction being caught red-handed will be washed over with shame—they know their partner is right. But emotionally immature people can't sit with that dose of shame—which is actually quite healthy for emotionally mature people to have when they know they did something wrong. So instead of saying something like "Yes, you are right, I feel ashamed about falling for the drink again. I'm committed to do better next time." and meaning it, they counterattack. "I drink because you can't stop nagging me. It's your fault that I feel desperate and misunderstood, so I drink!" Sentences like "You did this and this and that, and it's your fault that I feel this way." try to shift the burden of responsibility onto the other party. It is a form of gaslighting and a toxic thing to do. There's not to say that there may be no validity in the words of the attacker, but when they do it to counterattack someone who tries to hold them accountable, then it becomes deflection. They try to make everything to be the other person's fault.

The case of addicts and their partners is quite challenging as the partner can—understandably—become sarcastic, judgmental, or critical of the person who suffers from addiction, and this puts both of them in a vicious, codependent, reinforcing cycle which is very hard to escape. Judgment, sarcasm, and criticism are forms of defense mechanisms just as gaslighting and deflection are.

Shame is one of the most challenging emotions to sit with. With a lack of emotional maturity it transforms into anger and blame in the blink of an eye.

What Can You Do When Someone Drops a Shame Bomb on You in the Form of Criticism?

Hot cheeks, cold chill running through your body starting from your burning cheeks and down into your gut, foggy brain, feeling the need to just run... Familiar symptoms? When we get shamed we get flooded with a lot of uncomfortable physical symptoms that tell us to fly, fight, or freeze. What if you gave a different response next time? What if you could turn on your heels and make a different move?

Instead of retreating filled with fear, or working hard to explain yourself, what if you turned the tables? Shame and fear of messing up lead to dissociating from our empowered selves. We know that feeling; we know what it feels like when we're in that state of mind. What if you took that familiar state of mind and used it as a guide, a sign that it's time to pivot? Instead of your standard reaction of defense or withdrawal, what if you became the inquirer—and put the focus back on your criticizer by saying, "What do you mean?"

Asking someone what they mean with their criticism might not cross our mind, because we know all too well what these words they use mean. We've been criticized about that before. We can feel a physical pain when we think about the meaning of those words. All someone has to do is suggest that we are being that thing that triggers shame in us, and we're hijacked—agreeing with them on some level that we are in fact flawed.

Instead of immediately jumping on their train and agreeing with them, set aside all that you already know about being labeled (the pain, the physical symptoms, your previous association and meaning attached to the criticism) and ask them what they mean—and why they're saying what they're saying.

Especially if we're talking about different people who tell you the same criticism, they might mean something totally different than what you think. And secondly, what they actually mean may not be as bad as you think. The important part of all of this inquiring is to catch yourself when all your confidence is draining out of you, and then do something to get your power back.

Often it can turn out that certain labels mean totally different things to different people. Remember my story, when my new partner called me needy? I came from a relationship where that very concept of being emotionally needy and clingy was looked at with disdain. This further added to my own shame about being too vulnerable, wanting closeness, and longing for bonding. It was time for me to let go of that old story; the old story that says there's something wrong with me because I want to be loved and validated and close with my special people. Now I have someone in my life who is not going to participate in that old narrative, at all. To my partner the word needy held a neutral connotation, and when he said "Don't be needy." he used it in a humorous way that I couldn't understand for a moment, as every time I was being labeled needy before was a sharp criticism and an explicit word for a relationship deal breaker. If I had attracted another critical person into my life who condemned me for being needy, I might have to surmise that maybe I still needed to be taught some tough life lessons about this. The new critical person is there to reflect the shame the word "needy" brings up, so I need to work on the issue and get past it.

But thankfully, the opposite was true! I have a partner in my life who is totally okay with one of my least favorite traits… the "I'm too needy" trait. Which says that I'm probably getting really close to dropping that from my narrative about myself and I can heal.

When you get to a place with your bugaboo trait where people don't shame you for it and don't call you out because of it, and you don't take the label's eventual popping up to heart, congratulations! You just took a positive step forward in terms of facing head-on your shame-triggering quality.

The take-away from my story is to remember that you can always ask for more information from another person before deciding you know what they think and feel, especially if what you believe they think and feel is something that brings anxiety or fear.

The way of managing anxiety, especially the kind of anxiety that involves endless ruminating and obsessing, is simple: get more information. You may find yourself asking "What do you mean..." a lot going forward. And that's okay. It's a much better form of communication than jumping to conclusions and assuming you know, and then feeling bad about it.

By the way, anxiety...

Chapter 10: Anxiously Yours…

I felt anxious most of my life. Here is the fun fact about that: I couldn't even name it. I didn't know what anxiety was, but I did feel it. The problem with anxiety is not the emotion itself—that's completely manageable—but the lack of knowledge that surrounds it. In my family we didn't do anxiety. For my narrow-minded but very vocal father—and a bunch of other relatives—conditions different than high blood pressure, heart attack, stroke, and cancer were only the "inventions of weak people." Things such as ADHD, anxiety, or lactose and gluten intolerance were talked down upon. "Those are not real things. In my time none of these things existed and we were living just fine. Those whiny Americans invented all this BS."

No offense. For post-communist Eastern Europe everything magical and evil came from "America." There was no middle ground. Funnily enough, people could worship McDonalds and cuss "modern health problems" at the same time. Don't look for logic, there is none. This was true in my family's case, too. Me not being aware of something wooey-hooey called anxiety thus is not a surprise.

Mental health problems still get a harsher stigma than any physical condition—even in the most developed countries. No wonder people try to hide, downplay, or repress their mental issues. Anxiety disorder is largely the most common mental health problem. About 32% of the adult population in the United States experiences some kind of anxiety disorder during their lifetime.[xvii] So chances are high that someone sitting on the metro next to you has experienced anxiety in their lifetime. I think it's time to scrape off the stigma on anxiety—or any other mental health condition for that matter—and approach people with compassion and grace.

Growing up in a dysfunctional family increases our chances to experience anxiety during our lifetime. But it doesn't have to define our lives. Knowledge is the key to give our own definition to our lives. First, we need to know that this is a legitimate mental condition and there's nothing wrong with us if we have it. Anxiety always existed in humans, we just didn't know about it before; we didn't have the knowledge or the words to articulate it but that doesn't mean Julius Caesar or Fred Flintstone didn't suffer from it. You are not alone with it.

Until now I have been talking about anxiety as some kind of special mental condition. It can be, there are several levels of anxiety, but most of us only experience mild anxious episodes, which in fact are a normal condition of human existence.[xviii] When we give a talk, meet our crush, try to ask for a raise, or pass an exam, we might well experience anxiety. This emotional reaction makes sense, right? You allow yourself to feel it in such cases. But what about those cases when your anxiety doesn't make sense? When it hits you unexpectedly, yet it hurts you so you try to get rid of it in unhealthy ways? In this chapter I will help you to make sense and manage this type of mild to moderate anxiety. You do have power over your thoughts!

Have You Ever Thought about Murdering Someone?

Did I shock you with this question? I confess, I have. Think about murdering someone, that is. Hey, FBI, before you track me and arrest me as a raging, plotting serial murderer, hear me out.

When I'm stuck in traffic, my dad tells me to put on slippers, or I'm very angry about some random first-world problem, I think to myself, "I could kill that person!" Do I actually kill them? Hell no. I would never do that. But it sooths my overly charged emotional state to think these thoughts. It must be some evolutionary leftover from our caving forefathers.

My point is we don't always act on our thoughts. Heck, could you imagine that? People would murder, multiply, and empty stores of their Nutella stock everywhere. The world would be a Hobbesian anarchy and "Welcome to the Jungle" would be played on every radio station.

We don't listen to everything our mind conceives. We select which thoughts we want to listen to and which not to based on a variety of factors including our morals, values, and fears. Could we try to extend this selective listening to our anxiety-fueled thoughts too? Of course! Why not take this theory a step further? What if we could simultaneously stop acting on negative thoughts and change our thoughts to more constructive ones and act on those?

I didn't come up with this fantastic idea. It's part of cognitive behavioral therapy. CBT states that our emotions, thoughts, and actions are interconnected. And if we manage to change one of the three, the change will spill over to the other two areas.

In other words, if you can change your thoughts of a situation, you can also change your emotions and behavior in that situation. Would you act differently if you thought about yourself as a lovable human vs. an unlovable one? I'm sure you would.

If you change your behavior in a situation (for example, not acting out on your anxious, self-sabotaging thoughts) you can actually change your thoughts and emotions about that situation. Remember my story when I first discovered that I could actually let go of my snappy gut reaction to LE's hurtful words? That was the first moment I started shifting my thoughts about who I thought I was and later starting to feel better about the person I was.

Anxiety will probably always be a small part of your life. But the good news is that you can get really good at managing it and not letting it take over your thoughts or emotions.

Answer the following questions in your journal, or at least in your head:

- Try to pin down what happens to your relationship with yourself when you're getting into the "anxiety spiral"?

- What would happen if you looked at yourself in the mirror while you're feeling anxious, and said while maintaining eye contact, "Honey, what's the matter? You know I love you, right? You know you're lovable, right? Do you know I'm here for you?"

- How would you feel if you allowed yourself some self-nurturing and kind talk as you were spiraling into anxiety?

- What if you told yourself something along these lines: "You are an anxious, fearful little baby right now, and I love you anyway! You're worthy and lovable, and I don't care if you feel inadequate at the moment because I love you anyway."

Wouldn't it be nice to be treated so sweetly and kindly like that? You may know what it feels like to be on the receiving end of the opposite of such treatment as you were not pampered by your parents, you were victimized by someone. You can't undo that, but you can practice some healthy, corny self-love. And when you do it for yourself, when you hold yourself in such a regard, you won't settle for less. So you'll experience other people doing it for you, too.

When it comes to self-soothing it's okay to admit to yourself that you're being irrational, anxious, and insecure, but always add to the sentence that you love and accept yourself anyway. If you're thinking "I hate this about myself so much." you still have some healing work to do. The key is the "I love you anyway." part. It's pure self-acceptance.

Growing up in dysfunctional families, we may have felt ignored, unimportant, and invalidated, which may have triggered anxiety in us. No one signs up for such experiences by choice. These are terrible emotions to feel and they are dangerous because we can build an entire identity around them. What matters today, though, are the words you tell yourself about yourself from now or every time you are feeling these feelings.

Ask yourself: "Am I really that unworthy? Is this true?"

Name at least a few people in your life who care about you, who find you important, lovable. If you can't and these questions make you spiral even lower in your anxiety, switch strategies.

Ask yourself: "What's the best thing (the most loving, the most helpful, the most gracious, etc.) I can do today?"

Then do it. If you can't find your worth in thoughts, find it in actions.

SOS Anxiety Release

Sometimes anxiety can feel too overwhelming and seemingly impossible to manage. I like to use the metaphor of a drowning man. Whenever I feel anxiety too deeply I feel like drowning in an endless ocean, splashing around, trying to save myself, but there is nothing I can hang on to. In the past I worked so hard on getting rid of anxiety, I felt if I didn't escape this heavy emotion I'd die. So I focused on not dying instead of slowly and calmly making strokes towards the shore.

I'm not too anxious by default, but whenever I feel that I'm about to lose someone, I'm about to be abandoned or rejected, my anxiety kicks in full gear. It's not an unnatural reaction considering the fears I have. It's not the anxiety that is off base but my conclusion that all the fearful events I'm envisioning are actually going to happen.

When you're feeling like you're losing your power, you're losing control, you're losing ground, stop in whatever you're doing and ask yourself:

"Is this true? Is this fearful thing really happening to me? Or am I just assuming this is happening to me? How can I make sure what I think is true? Where can I get the information needed to know for sure?"

In most cases, you'll realize that your assumptions are nothing more than assumptions and most of the things your catastrophizing mind created never actually happened.

Another great technique to release anxiety is belly breathing. How do you do it? Place one hand on your belly, close your eyes, and slowly start inhaling through your nostrils, noting, "Breathing in—I'm aware of breathing in." Drive your in breath deep into your belly, feeling as it expands, and notice your palm rising. Hold your breath for three to five seconds and then slowly start exhaling from your mouth, noting, "Breathing out—I'm aware of breathing out."

Repeat this exercise for five to ten minutes. Try to keep your mind focused on your expanding and shrinking belly, or your raising and falling palms, notice when you breathe in and out. When you're done, take a second to assess how you feel. Do you feel calmer?

When we feel anxious, our heart rate rises and our breathing becomes more shallow. Some people hyperventilate. These are the typical symptoms of sensing danger so they prepare the body for fight-or-flight mode. Slow and deep breaths, in contrast, mimic a state of tranquility; they sooth the mind. Adrenaline slowly burns away in your body, your heart rate drops, and you regain composure. While belly breathing sounds like new age witchcraft, it's actually simple biology.

A Final Thought...

Emotional maturity is a truly life-changing quality to master. With that comes self-worth, self-acceptance, and self-love. It's really important for you to always remember how valuable you are and what you bring to the table.

"Okay, how can I make sure that people can see how valuable I am?" The answer to that lies in making sure that you yourself are aware of the value that you bring. If you are aware of and placing value on your worth, and acknowledging that whoever you are is valuable, then you will conduct yourself in a way where people will pick up on it too.

Being aware of the value of your authentic self is not about becoming demanding and loudly telling everyone, "Don't you see what values I have, how good I am?" It's more of an attitude... or a belief system from which you operate. I don't know much about you as I've never met you in person. But for sure I know this about you: You have a growth mindset and a genuine wish to become your best self. And that's huge. If you feel someone's not seeing your inner light and you start to feel discouraged, say to yourself: "I realize that relationships involve great joy but also compromise, and even sacrifice. People have to meet in the middle and have to make changes to accommodate the other sometimes. And because I put a great emphasis on my self-knowledge and self-worth I can accommodate my partner and I can lead an authentic life by example. This is a gift to anyone. Not every relationship partner can offer that, but that's what I bring to the table. And as this is important to me, I won't settle if someone doesn't value, appreciate, or see that in me."

A word of caution, though. You may become your most honest and open and vulnerable self, the real, authentic you. You may know your issues, your origin story, why you behaved in a certain way, how you dealt with your emotional baggage, and so on. But expecting everyone else to be like that is not something you want to do.

Also, just because you can be self-reflective—whereas many people are not—doesn't mean it's the best thing to share your most authentic self and truth with everyone. That level of vulnerability and openness only belongs in a safe place, where the recipient has proven that they will hold dear any information you share. They will not use it against you. They will not exploit you or manipulate you. They must earn it before you give it. Also, they must demonstrate a genuine interest in knowing your open and vulnerable side. Give them time and opportunity to express that interest. Watch and listen for it. If it is never there, then don't divulge all your inner truths.

So in conversations, especially ones that are deep and self-disclosing, you want to take turns—keep sharing things somewhat equal. Share a little and let them share a little, then you share a little more and wait so that they can catch up and share a little more, and so on. If they stop revealing and disclosing, maybe it's time to put a cap on the vulnerable stuff until some other time when you're both participating in the same way. It's a matter of keeping things in balance, and not moving faster or deeper than the stage of the relationship indicates. This way you won't feel that you're putting more in the relationship, that you're more interested than the other person, so your anxiety about being inadequate will subside.

Emotional maturity has to do a lot with self-reflection, understanding your needs, and understanding the needs of others, too. When we operate from a premise of awareness and we take action based on the values of our best selves (instead of our fears, anxieties, and lacking) we will be the masters of our destiny. Because we do have control over it.

I wish you the best journey!

Love,
Zoe

Before You Go...

How did you like Find How To Be Whole Again? Would you consider leaving a feedback about your reading experience so other readers could know about it? If you are willing to sacrifice some of your time to do so, there are several options you can do it:

1. Leave a review on Amazon

2. Leave a review on goodreads.com. Here is a link to my profile where you find all of my books.
https://www.goodreads.com/author/show/14967542.Zoe_McKey

3. Send me a private message to zoemckey@gmail.com

4. Tell your friends and family about your reading experience.

Your feedback is very valuable to me to assess if I'm on the good path providing help to you and where do I need to improve. Your feedback is also valuable to other people as they can learn about my work and perhaps give an independent author as myself a chance. I deeply appreciate any kind of feedback you take time to provide me.

Thank you so much for choosing to read my book among the many out there. If you'd like to receive an update once I have a new book, you can subscribe to my newsletter at www.zoemckey.com. You'll get My Daily Routine Makeover cheat sheet and Unbreakable Confidence checklist for FREE. You'll also get occasional book recommendations from other authors I trust and know they deliver good quality books.

Brave Enough

Time to learn how to overcome the feeling of inferiority and achieve success. Brave Enough takes you step by step through the process of understanding the nature of your fears, overcome limiting beliefs and gain confidence with the help of studies, personal stories and actionable exercises at the end of each chapter.

Say goodbye to fear of rejection and inferiority complex once and for all.

Less Mess Less Stress

Don't compromise with your happiness. "Good enough" is not the life you deserve - you deserve the best, and the good news is that you can have it. Learn the surprising truth that it's not by doing more, but less with Less Mess Less Stress.

We know that we own too much, we say yes for too many engagements, and we stick to more than we should. Physical, mental and relationship clutter are daily burdens we have to deal with. Change your mindset and live a happier life with less.

Minimalist Budget

Minimalist Budget will help you to turn your bloated expenses into a well-toned budget, spending on exactly what you need and nothing else.

This book presents solutions for two major problems in our consumer society: (1) how to downsize your cravings without having to sacrifice the fun stuff, and (2) how to whip your finances into shape and follow a personalized budget.

Rewire Your Habits

Rewire Your Habits discusses which habits one should adopt to make changes in 5 life areas: self-improvement, relationships, money management, health, and free time. The book addresses every goal-setting, habit building challenge in these areas and breaks them down with simplicity and ease.

Tame Your Emotions

Tame Your Emotions is a collection of the most common and painful emotional insecurities and their antidotes. Even the most successful people have fears and self-sabotaging habits. But they also know how to use them to their advantage and keep their fears on a short leash. This is exactly what my book will teach you – using the tactics of experts and research-proven methods.

Emotions can't be eradicated. But they can be controlled.

The Art of Minimalism

The Art of Minimalism will present you 4 minimalist techniques, the bests from around the world, to give you a perspective on how to declutter your house, your mind, and your life in general. Learn how to let go of everything that is not important in your life and find methods that give you a peace of mind and happiness instead.

Keep balance at the edge of minimalism and consumerism.

The Critical Mind

If you want to become a critical, effective, and rational thinker instead of an irrational and snap-judging one, this book is for you. Critical thinking skills strengthen your decision making muscle, speed up your analysis and judgment, and help you spot errors easily.

The Critical Mind offers a thorough introduction to the rules and principles of critical thinking. You will find widely usable and situation-specific advice on how to critically approach your daily life, business, friendships, opinions, and even social media.

The Disciplined Mind

Where you end up in life is determined by a number of times you fall and get up, and how much pain and discomfort you can withstand along the way. The path to an extraordinary accomplishment and a life worth living is not innate talent, but focus, willpower, and disciplined action.

Maximize your brain power and keep in control of your thoughts.

In The Disciplined Mind, you will find unique lessons through which you will learn those essential steps and qualities that are needed to reach your goals easier and faster.

The Mind-Changing Habit of Journaling

Understand where your negative self-image, bad habits, and unhealthy thoughts come from. Know yourself to change yourself. Embrace the life-changing transformation potential of journaling. This book shows you how to use the ultimate self-healing tool of journaling to find your own answers to your most pressing problems, discover your true self and lead a life of growth mindset.

The Unlimited Mind

This book collects all the tips, tricks and tactics of the most successful people to develop your inner smartness.

The Unlimited Mind will show you how to think smarter and find your inner genius. This book is a collection of research and scientific studies about better decision-making, fairer judgments, and intuition improvement. It takes a critical look at our everyday cognitive habits and points out small but serious mistakes that are easily correctable.

Who You Were Meant To Be

Discover the strengths of your personality and how to use them to make better life choices. In Who You Were Born To Be, you'll learn some of the most influential personality-related studies. Thanks to these studies you'll learn to capitalize on your strengths, and how you can you become the best version of yourself.

Wired For Confidence

Do you feel like you just aren't good enough? End this vicious thought cycle NOW. Wired For Confidence tells you the necessary steps to break out from the pits of low self-esteem, lowered expectations, and lack of assertiveness.

Take the first step to creating the life you only dared to dream of.

References

Ambardar, Sheenie. Narcissistic Personality Disorder. Medscape. 2018. https://emedicine.medscape.com/article/1519417-overview#a5

Chalquist, Craig. A Glossary of Freudian Terms 2001. Retrieved on 4 January 2020.

Gibson, Lindsay C. Adult Children of Emotionally Immature Parents. New Harbinger Publications. 2015.

Gibson, Lindsay. Dr. Emotional loneliness. Dr. Lindsey Gibson. 2015. http://www.drlindsaygibson.com/articles/emotional-loneliness

Hendriksen, Ellen. "Is Your Relationship Codependent? And What Exactly Does That Mean?". Scientific American. Scientific American. Retrieved 4 January 2020.

Johnson, R. Skip (13 July 2014). "Codependency and Codependent Relationships". BPDFamily.com. Retrieved 5 January 2020.

Landa, S; Duschinsky, R (2013), "Crittenden's dynamic–maturational model of attachment and adaptation", Review of General Psychology, 17 (3): 326–338, doi:10.1037/a0032102

Liem, Joan H.; Boudewyn, Arne C. (1999). "Contextualizing the effects of childhood sexual abuse on adult self- and social functioning: an attachment theory perspective". Child Abuse & Neglect. 23 (11): 1141–1157. doi:10.1016/S0145-2134(99)00081-2.

Mayo Clinic Staff. Narcissistic Personality Disorder. Mayo Clinic. 2020. https://www.mayoclinic.org/diseases-conditions/narcissistic-personality-disorder/symptoms-causes/syc-20366662

McLoad, Saul. Defense Mechanisms. Simply Psyhology. 2019. https://www.simplypsychology.org/defense-mechanisms.html

Mirzaei, M., Yasini Ardekani, S. M., Mirzaei, M., & Dehghani, A. (2019). Prevalence of Depression, Anxiety and Stress among Adult Population: Results of Yazd Health Study.

Iranian journal of psychiatry, 14(2), 137–146.
https://www.ncbi.nlm.nih.gov/pmc/articles/PMC6702282/

Ni, Preston. M.S.B.A. 6 Common Traits of Narcissists and Gaslighters. Psychology Today. 2017.
https://www.psychologytoday.com/intl/blog/communication-success/201707/6-common-traits-narcissists-and-gaslighters

Sane Australia. Narcissistic Personality Disorder. Sane Australia. 2020.
https://www.sane.org/information-stories/facts-and-guides/narcissistic-personality-disorder

Smith, Eliot R.; Mackie, Diane M. (2007). Social Psychology (3rd ed.). Psychology Press. ISBN 9781841694092.

Van Buren, A.; Cooley, E.L. (Dec 2002). "Attachment Styles, View of Self and Negative Affect". North American Journal of Psychology. 4 (3): 417–430. ISSN 1527-7143. Retrieved 9 January 2020.

Van Dijk, Sheri. Calming the Emotional Storm. New Harbinger Publications. 2012.

Waters, E.; Corcoran, D.; Anafarta, M. (2005). "Attachment, Other Relationships, and the Theory That All Good Things Go Together".

Human Development. 48 (1–2): 80–84. doi:10.1159/000083217.

Endnotes

[i] Gibson, Lindsay. Dr. Emotional loneliness. Dr. Lindsey Gibson. 2015. http://www.drlindsaygibson.com/articles/emotional-loneliness

[ii] Gibson, Lindsay C. Adult Children of Emotionally Immature Parents. New Harbinger Publications. 2015.

[iii] Chalquist, Craig. A Glossary of Freudian Terms 2001. Retrieved on 4 January 2020.

[iv] Chalquist, Craig. A Glossary of Freudian Terms 2001. Retrieved on 4 January 2020.

[v] McLoad, Saul. Defense Mechanisms. Simply Psyhology. 2019. https://www.simplypsychology.org/defense-mechanisms.html

[vi] Smith, Eliot R.; Mackie, Diane M. (2007). Social Psychology (3rd ed.). Psychology Press. ISBN 9781841694092.

[vii] Johnson, R. Skip (13 July 2014). "Codependency and Codependent Relationships". BPDFamily.com. Retrieved 5 January 2020.

[viii] Hendriksen, Ellen. "Is Your Relationship Codependent? And What Exactly Does That Mean?". Scientific American. Scientific American. Retrieved 4 January 2020.

[ix] Ambardar, Sheenie. Narcissistic Personality Disorder. Medscape. 2018. https://emedicine.medscape.com/article/1519417-overview#a5

[x] Sane Australia. Narcissistic Personality Disorder. Sane Australia. 2020. https://www.sane.org/information-stories/facts-and-guides/narcissistic-personality-disorder

[xi] Mayo Clinic Staff. Narcissistic Personality Disorder. Mayo Clinic. 2020.

https://www.mayoclinic.org/diseases-conditions/narcissistic-personality-disorder/symptoms-causes/syc-20366662

[xii] Ni, Preston. M.S.B.A. 6 Common Traits of Narcissists and Gaslighters. Psychology Today. 2017. https://www.psychologytoday.com/intl/blog/communication-success/201707/6-common-traits-narcissists-and-gaslighters

[xiii] Waters, E.; Corcoran, D.; Anafarta, M. (2005). "Attachment, Other Relationships, and the Theory That All Good Things Go Together". Human Development. 48 (1–2): 80–84. doi:10.1159/000083217.

[xiv] Landa, S; Duschinsky, R (2013), "Crittenden's dynamic–maturational model of attachment and adaptation", Review of General Psychology, 17 (3): 326–338, doi:10.1037/a0032102

[xv] Van Buren, A.; Cooley, E.L. (Dec 2002). "Attachment Styles, View of Self and Negative

Affect". North American Journal of Psychology. 4 (3): 417–430. ISSN 1527-7143. Retrieved 9 January 2020.

[xvi] Liem, Joan H.; Boudewyn, Arne C. (1999). "Contextualizing the effects of childhood sexual abuse on adult self- and social functioning: an attachment theory perspective". Child Abuse & Neglect. 23 (11): 1141–1157. doi:10.1016/S0145-2134(99)00081-2.

[xvii] Mirzaei, M., Yasini Ardekani, S. M., Mirzaei, M., & Dehghani, A. (2019). Prevalence of Depression, Anxiety and Stress among Adult Population: Results of Yazd Health Study. Iranian journal of psychiatry, 14(2), 137–146. https://www.ncbi.nlm.nih.gov/pmc/articles/PMC6702282/

[xviii] Van Dijk, Sheri. Calming the Emotional Storm. New Harbinger Publications. 2012.

Printed in Great Britain
by Amazon